BEST OF BLOOPERS

KERMIT SCHAFER'S

BEST OF

BLOOPERS

AVENEL BOOKS · NEW YORK

DEDICATION

This book is dedicated as a sympathetic tribute to members of the broadcasting industry who have been the victims of Bloopers, in the hope that it offers consolation and proof of the fact that they are not alone.

To err is human,
To forgive, divine.
Alexander Pope

To forgive is human,
To err, divine.
Kermit Schafer

BEST OF BLOOPERS

Pick Me Up

On New Year's Eve, Johnny Carson's "Tonight Show" participated in NBC-TV festivities, which included mobile unit pickups from the Times Square area. In the spirit of the evening Johnny told his viewers, "We now switch you to 42nd Street and Broadway for a Times Square pickup."

A Slip on the Ice

In a recent weather report which described the snowfall in the Northwest, the announcer on KHAR, Alaska, said: "And Helena got six inches during the night . . . Helena, Montana, that is!"

Really Big

NEWSCASTER: "Beautiful Raquel Welch has won the Inter-State Theatre Star of the 60's Award and the 1967 International Star of the Year from Cinerama and Pacific Theatres. Miss Welch is the proud owner of two really big ones."

Family Planning

COMMERCIAL: "So, remember . . . Goodyear four-ply rubber to help prevent families . . . I mean Goodyear rubber tires to help your family prevent accidents!"

Horse Opera

The following commercial was heard over a Philadelphia radio station: "You already know of Aquarama in Philadelphia and the fine entertainment they have there. But I want to tell you of a spectacular they are having on this coming Friday night. For the first time in history, I repeat, for the first time in history . . . see a man rape a horse! Oh, my goodness! I'm sorry . . . for the first time in history see a man race a porpoise . . . Uncle Philsie will be there if he can make it after this."

Father Knows Best

At one point during the coverage of the Republican National Convention which originated from Miami Beach, Florida, a TV camera was taking candid shots of delegates who were in the audience. The camera singled out a very pregnant lady in the audience who was spotted standing directly in front of a large poster which read, "NIXON IS THE ONE!"

No Comment

An announcer, reading it right off the wire: "A severe storm hit Atlantic City, New Jersey, today, bringing high winds, hail, and more than two inches of rain. A sailor was sucked under the boardwalk by a big Wave!"

On Thin Ice

Ed Sullivan told about some of the winter sports athletes he was going to have on his show: "Among them will be the world *sholom* champion."

Situation Wanted

The disc jockey of radio station KOLO, Reno, Nevada, announced the next number to be played on his program: "A Hard Man is Good to Find."

Slip of the Tongue

A disk jockey closing up a late music show said, "We've got just enough time to slip into April Stevens."

Everything Is Coming Up Roses

The commercial was usually stated like this: ". . . So, try Rosedale's flavor of the month, strawberry ripple ice cream." But when the announcer picked it up to read it, this is what the radio listeners heard: ". . . So, try Rosedale's *monthly flavor*, strawberry ripple ice cream."

Good Night, Ladies

In Northbay, Canada, a radio announcer opened his morning show "To the Ladies" by saying, "And now, this number I dedicate to all you newlyweds." He played: "It Only Hurts for a Little While."

Water Boy

The following was heard on a Sacramento, California, FM radio station: "This mellowed beer is brewed with pukey mountain water . . . *pure* Rocky Mountain water!"

Love at First Sight

When I appeared with Merv Griffin as the guest on his new late-night show on CBS-TV, Merv related this blooper on the air. "On the first day of my new afternoon show, I couldn't wait to see who our first sponsor was. It turned out to be a well-known laxative. I eagerly said, 'Well . . . we're off and running.' "

Full Moon Shot

ANNOUNCER: "Stay tuned to NBC for the Apollo *Luny* Landing! . . . *LUNAR!*"

Small Talk

"We will return to the story of the Seven Dwarfs after a pause for a short sponsor's message."

Another First

Christiaan Barnard, prominent surgeon, is here to address a medical convention about his now-famous rear transplant . . . of course . . . I mean *rare* transplant."

Hooked

"See a CBS special on marijuana . . . get the habit, stay tuned to this channel."

Quick on the Drawers

On "The Newlywed Game," the host asked a husband the question "What one thing did it take your wife a few days to get used to doing after marrying you?"
He thought a while and answered, "Oh, I'd have to say going into my drawers." The audience roared. He then said, "Oh, you know, *dresser* drawers!"

No News Is Good News

A newscaster reported in full detail an automobile accident in which the driver lost control of her car on a curve, crashed through the guardrail, and rolled down a steep embankment. She was understandably shaken by this experience but luckily suffered no serious injuries. At this point, the newscaster enthusiastically related the lady's efforts to climb the embankment and obtain aid. He emphatically announced, "As she reached the highway, she climaxed . . . er, *collapsed!*"

5

Total Recall

Walter Cronkite was reading the news about Rolls-Royce having a recall campaign, when he said, "Rolls-Royce announced today that it is recalling all Rolls-Royce cars made after 1966 because of faulty nuts behind the steering wheels."

Take Him Over the Coals

On Station CJOH, Ottawa, Canada, during the 11:00 P.M. news, Larry Henderson (the news commentator), talking about the Pope lighting the new fire for Easter, said, "The fire was lit in a brassiere . . . I beg your pardon, I mean *brazier!*"

Double Jeopardy

Art Fleming of "Jeopardy" should have been awarded a medal for composure for his recent stone-faced performance on this one: In question to the answer "A decorative section of the bowsprit on sailing vessels," a young lady replied, "What is a maidenhead?"

Small Kraft Warning

Announcer Ed Herlihy blooped: "Another delicious combination for these hot days, also by Kraft, is a chilled grease sandwich and a choke!"

Nipped in the Bud

On the last day of "The Merv Griffin Show" for Westinghouse, Merv was introducing fourteen-year-old singer Julie Budd. Talking about old times, Merv came out with this blooper: "Since we discovered Julie when she was twelve, she really developed (*chuckles from audience*). Oh, come on," Merv replied.

For Pete's Sake

NEWSCASTER: "Now, briefly *recrapping* the news . . . On Capitol Hill, G-O-Lee peters . . . ."

For Men Only

PUBLIC SERVICE ANNOUNCEMENT: *"Residents of this city are urged to show up at the County Whore House for their polio shots . . . I beg your pardon, that should read County Court House."*

Ouch!

ANNOUNCER: "This portion of 'Rawhide' is brought to you by Vaseline Petroleum Jelly!"

Sticky Stuff

LOCAL NEWS: "So, remember . . . we want all of you to turn out for the Peter pulling contest at St. Taffy's Church . . . ugh . . . that should be the *taffy* pulling contest at St. *Peter's* Church this Sunday!"

Could Be

This happened during a children's program patterned after what Art Linkletter does when he talks to kids on his television show.

The emcee asked a little second-grade girl what her favorite subject in school was. The little girl replied gym class. When asked what she did in gym class, she said play games and kick balls around. The emcee came back with: "That will come in handy when you are dating."

Fun and Games

The following was heard on KNOW Radio in Austin, Texas. A sportscaster, while preparing to announce the baseball scores, said . . . "And now, for the gay dames—I mean—the *day's games.*"

Hard Line

Heard on the TV soap opera "As the World Turns": "Yes, sir, he is very long to get a hard with . . . hard to get along with."

Chinese Yen

LOCAL NEWS: "And still missing in the unsolved Bache robbery is a million dollars worth of blue chop sticks!"

Nature in the Raw

On Art Linkletter's kid show, he asked a little girl what she would buy if she had ten dollars. This was her reply. "I would buy my parents some pajamas, because they sleep together without any clothes on!"

Are You Smoking More and Enjoying It Less?

Mel Allen, ace sportscaster, interviewed an all-America football player on his program following the Pabst Blue Ribbon fights on CBS. Mel always made a habit of offering his sponsor's cigars to his guests. However, the football great threw Mel a curve when he pushed a box of cigars aside and said, "I never touch those things, they make me sick!"

So I Ain't Neat

INTERVIEWER: "Doris Day, I've seen your new picture 'Young At Heart,' and I think it's simply wonderful!"
DORIS DAY: "That's great, except we haven't even started shooting, 'Young At Heart' yet!"

That's the Living End

On WHAT'S MY LINE?, Dorothy Kilgallen, famous columnist, introduced a guest panelist in this classic fashion. "Arlene Francis is on a much-deserved vacation in New England tonight, but she left part of her behind, Martin Gabel!"

Ben Who?

Veteran announcer Ben Grauer was announcing for the NBC symphony. "You have been listening to a program of symphonic music by the New York Philharmonic orchestra under the baton of Atosco Touranini . . . ah . . . Otosco Tiscanini . . . that's Arturo Toscanini. Well. Your announcer has been Ben Grauer, ladies and gentlemen. Remember the name— you may never hear it again!"

Dark Victory

On a post-game telecast at San Diego, Los Angeles Dodger announcer Jerry Doggit was talking to Wes Parker who won the ball game on a triple. All of a sudden the lights went out. Jerry said, "Hey, Buzzie, turn the lights on, we didn't mean it. Oh, well, I guess we'll have to do our thing in the dark!"

Rhodes Scholar

Governor James A. Rhodes and President Johnson helped Ohio University in Athens observe its 160th anniversary on May 7, 1964. Governor Rhodes got tangled up on the word "heartily" and said "heartedly." This apparently threw his next phrase. He intended to say this "venerable institution," but it came out "this *venereal* institution."

Half Time

STATION BREAK: "We will reurn to the third half of 'The Virginian' in just a moment."

Coming Up Next!

Public Service Announcement! The following went out on all fifty thousand glorious watts: ". . . To qualify for President Johnson's All American Team, all you have to do is perform a series of sit-ups, push-ups, and *throw-ups!*"

Blue Monday

Scene: "The Garry Moore Show" (in the morning) about five years ago.

Animal-man Ivan T. Sanderson has brought in a gopher and has delivered his spiel. Garry is attempting to get the gopher to perform in some manner—to rear upon its hind legs. Finally, Garry resorts to lifting the gopher's tail and blowing air on its fanny, trying to rouse it to action. Garry blurts out: "What a way to spend a Monday morning—blowing a gopher!"

Time to Retire

The long hours of the Apollo moon landing began to tell on veteran newsman Walter Cronkite when he told his millions of viewers that "Blast-off was scheduled at 11:00 P.OFF . . P.M.!"

The Eyes of Texas

NEWSCASTER: "These Federal funds are being used in the United States, also in Texas."

For Pete's Sake

On a Joey Bishop show Sammy Davis, Jr., and Peter Lawford came on to plug their movie *Salt and Pepper*. When it came time to show a film clip of the movie, Joey announced, "And now for a few scenes from the new movie *Salt and Peter!*" Everyone broke up, including Joey.

Pained Remark

On the Pocket Billiards show "Ten-Twenty," one of the contestants wished to have the billiard balls set up. Joe Wilson, describing the action, said: "At this point Mr. Crane asks the referee to rack his balls!"

Real George

On "This Morning," an ABC conversation program, host Dick Cavett's guest was Christine Jorgenson (once George Jorgenson), who was discussing her transferal of sexes. She explained that there were eight or more different places in the body where sex is determined. "Sex is not determined by genitals alone."

Whereupon the host came out with, "I don't quite think I grasp that . . . I'm sorry, that's an awful thing to say." The entire studio broke up with laughter.

Take Me Out to the Ball Game

The following occurred on "The Yankee Wrap-up," following the New York–Baltimore game. Jerry Coleman was interviewing two of the ballplayers' wives; he was curious about how the family functioned when the husbands are on the road.

WIFE: When he's away, I have to take charge of everything. I have to be pretty much the man in the family.

COLEMAN: Yes, I suppose you do have to wear the pants in the family at that time.

WIFE: Yes, but when he comes home, I take them off.

True or False

Allen Ludden on "Password" asked Juliet Prowse which imitation in her night club act she liked the most.

"Mae West," was Juliet's reply.

Allen remarked that she wore a padded dress for this, which looks very realistic. "But it's not the Juliet I know," Allen commented *(audience laughter)*.

"Oh, really?" asked Juliet.

Broad Statement

PUBLIC SERVICE ANNOUNCEMENT: *"It's three P.M. Eastern Standard Time, and time for Brenda Bradley, our Community Bulletin Broad."*

So Solly

On an Armed Forces radio program in Tokyo the announcer was reviewing coming special events for the week. Here is how an art exhibit was publicized: "18 works of the late Goyo Hashiguchi (1880-1921) will be introduced at the International House of Japan from November 17th to the 19th. From 1915 until his premature death in 1912 . . ." He never did catch his mistake.

Dead Pigeon

FIRST ACTOR: "What are you in jail for? . . . I'm in for petty larceny."
SECOND ACTOR: "I'm in for armed robbery . . . some dirty squeal pigeon stooled on me!"

On the Spot

NEWSCASTER: "This is your eleven o'clock newscaster bringing you an on the pot report . . . I mean on the spot retort. . . . I mean on the tot resort . . . oh well, let's just skip it!"

Things Are Rough All Over

NEWSCASTER: "And here is further news on that rape case. All the victim could tell police officials was that her attacker wore rough levi pants."

Navy Blue

ANNOUNCER: "This is a public service announcement. Attention all student nurses. From Washington comes the announcement that the Navy Department is now giving instructions in special new curses for Navy nurses."

How About That!

Mel Allen was guilty of a blooper during a New York Yankee broadcast. He said, "Remember, tomorrow night is Ladies' Night—just fifty cents for all the ladies."

Unfare Remark

Comedienne Carol Burnett has made it a practice to interview people in her audience as part of her own "Carol Burnett" TV program. On one occasion she chatted with a cab driver who enthusiastically told her and her network TV audience that he "had her in my taxi!"

Virgin Territory

Singer Kaye Stevens, making her first TV appearance on the "Jack Paar" late night show, was obviously very nervous after her debut. Paar asked her if this was truly her first appearance on television, to which she replied, "I was a virgin until I appeared on your program, Mr. Paar!"

All Mixed Up

While talking to people in his studio audience, Steve Allen searched for two girls who had sent a note to him stating that King Size and Regular were in his audience. In asking where they were seated, he said, "While I still remember, where are King Size and Cork Tip?"
As a gift he gave the 5-foot 11-inch girl an electric fan, and the shorter girl a Waring Mixor. He always emphasizes the word mixor, not mixer. He said it was a hand mixor: "It mixes hands so well you can never straighten them . . . they now make mixors for His and Hores!"

Chow

Spacecaster: "Apollo Astronauts Armstrong, Aldrin, and Collins have received a 'go' for lunch . . . *launch!*"

Good Sports

NEWSCASTER: "Miss Lesley Bush of Princeton, New Jersey, and Charlie Hickcox of Phoenix, Arizona, both Olympic Gold Medal winners, will be married Saturday at Bloomington.

"They will spend their honeymoon in an AAU sponsored exhibition in Montevideo, Uruguay."

Girl Talk

"For excitement and beautiful girls see color *cleverage* of the Rose Bowl Game New Year's Day on CBS."

Bedtime Story

On "The Joey Bishop Show," Senator Barry Goldwater had been asked by Joey if he would like to be on the show twice a week. The senator replied, "No, thank you, I'd much rather watch you in bed with my wife."

I Never Remember a Face

ANNOUNCER: "See a TV special—the Russian Bolshoi Ballet in a never-to-be remembered performance Sunday at nine."

Answer Yes or No

David Frost had F. Lee Bailey as his guest. They were discussing Truman Capote's book *In Cold Blood*. David turned to his studio audience, and asked, how many of you read the film or saw the book?

Testy

A newscaster on KFRU in Columbia, Missouri, began a news-cast with this: "Magistrate Judge Temple Morgett set Wednesday as the final day for lawyers to file their briefs in the case of a local man arrested for drunken driving who refused to take a breast test . . . *breath* test!"

Inspirational Message

Following the sermonette that closed the regular TV programming for the day on a Palm Springs, California, TV station, late viewers were treated to a showing of stag movies that were being screened by a station employee. This engineering blooper resulted in an avalanche of phone calls, many of which requested a rerun of the films.

A Ding a Ling

During one of Steve Allen's shows he kept substituting the word "dingdong" for other words. He had on this particular show a culinary expert to whom Steve said, "The way to a man's heart is through his *dingdong.*" It should have been stomach, of course.

Peep Show

During television coverage of a political convention some years ago, NBC-TV was using a new camera called "the creepy peepie" to cover the events on the convention floor. During a station break an announcer on one of our local stations encouraged us to "get full convention coverage with NBC and its creepy *people.*"

Call a Cop

On local radio station WAOK in Rhode Island, when a disc jockey was advertising the YMCA Fair, he said, "Children under twelve must be accomplished by an adult . . . uh . . . er . . . that is, children must be *accompanied* by an adult under twelve years of age."

He's Got to Go

Johnny Carson said on "The Tonight Show": "Here's how to relieve an upsex stomach . . . I mean an *upsep* stomach . . . with Sex Lax . . . *Ex-lax!*"

Party Girl

Comedian Marty Ingels appeared as a guest on "The Steve Allen Show." Steve's wife, Jayne Meadows, also appeared on the program. Jayne got all fouled up when she told Steve, "I knew that Marty was the type to have a child . . . I saw him at a party recently [audience laughter] . . . well, you know what I mean."

Sick Commercial

COMMERCIAL: "So try Vick's 44 Cough Syrup and we guarantee that you'll never get any better!"

On the Make

Heard on "What's My Line."
BENNETT CERF: "Is the product made in Hollywood?"
ARLENE FRANCIS: "Isn't everybody?"

Ready Eddy

Ed Sullivan, closing out his Sunday night TV program, found a few seconds to do a quick public service message. He closed his show, "And now a word about tuberculosis . . . Good night, everybody . . . help stamp out *TV!*"

No Comment

NEWSCASTER: ". . . and here is more concerning the Pope's current condition following the surgical removal of his prostate: It has been learned that the fountains in Vatican Square have been ordered turned off because it had been feared that the sound of running water would bother the Pope."

Be My Guest

ANNOUNCER: "Good evening, this is your musicologist, Fred Laney. Tonight's program features music for ancient instruments and sopranos. Tonight's guest is ancient soprano, Viola Finkleoffer."

Burp

NEWSCASTER: "President Johnson and Premier Kosygin are now having luncheon comprising a typical American meal in Gasboro, New Jersey . . . that should be Glassboro . . . and now a word from Alka Seltzer!"

Even Your Best Friend Won't Tell You

ANNOUNCER: "Go to your neighborhood theatre to see Rita Hayworth, whose Salami will take your breath away . . . that should be Salome."

It's Worth a Try

During the Pueblo spy ship crisis NBC news commentator Pauline Fredericks was broadcasting a special U.N. news summary. This summary occurred on a Saturday morning, when many kids shows were pre-empted. She told her viewers that ". . . Canada was helping decide whether the U.N. will send (KIDS SHOW CUT IN) the Cub Scouts!"

Shaggy Dog Story

On the NBC "Today" show, newscaster Merrill Mueller did the commercial lead-in for Alpo Dog Food thus: "I see Hugh Downs is keeping some shady lady lately . . . I mean some shaggy company lately . . . I mean a shaggy dog lately!"

He Must Be Choking

Curt Gowdy, during the broadcast of a World Series game between the Boston Red Sox and the St. Louis Cardinals and also during a football game between the San Diego Chargers and the Oakland Raiders, observed: "Folks, this is perfect weather for today's game. Not a breath of air."

Just Reward

Comedians Don Rickles and Red Buttons appeared as guests on the "Mike Douglas Show." Rickles was singing the praises of a Danny Thomas-produced program entitled "Zero Man." In his enthusiasm for the program Rickles inadvertently said, "I wouldn't be a bit surprised if Danny Thomas got an Enema Award for this one."

Food for Thought

NEWSCASTER: "This controversial pill will be checked by the Pure Dude and Fugg Administration."

He's Working on a New Case

NEWSCASTER: "Stay tuned to ABC-TV's 'Good Company' celebrity interview program, starring F. Lee Bailey, prominent lawyer known throughout the bars of the nation."

So What Else Is New?

On the Bob and Ray Show of several years ago Ray had on an apron as he was demonstrating how to make a fancy octopus salad. He had the body of an octopus before him and as he laid the carrot curls around it he said, ". . . and these, ladies, are the testicles!" *SILENCE . . . SILENCE . . . AND MORE SILENCE.*

Fair Enough

WEATHER FORECST: "This is your weather girl bringing you the forecast for eastern Texas and vicinity, direct from the airport. Today's forecast is for fair and mild with a pleasant weekend in prospect for you golfers and fishermen. (LOUD CLAP OF THUNDER) Oh, oh . . . you had better bring your rubbers."

The Rain In Spain

During a roundtable TV discussion that centered around *My Fair Lady* one of the participants said that the climax of the play occurred when the stars decided to marry. Others said that it occurred earlier. The moderator, in pointing out that the climax was seen earlier in the play, mentioned that the marriage was really anticlimactic, then added, "Don't think that I mean that marriage is an anticlimax, there are many climaxes in marriage (FLUSTERED) . . . well, that is . . . well, I am sure that you all know what I mean."

A Lot of Guts

SPORTSCASTER: "Davis Cup Tennis Star Fred Perry severely sprained his leg and it is feared that he might have served a nerve, I mean, severed!"

Hostess with the Mostest

Oleg Cassini did the commentary on a fashion show he presented on Johnny Carson's "The Tonight Show." He described a gown worn by one of his models in this way: "This is a lovely hostess dinner dress with a very low neckline for easy entertaining."

The Old Gray Mare

A youngster told Art Linkletter that he watched a milkman's parked horse for a while and figured out that the animal was stuck because "it just lost all of its gasoline."

Doctor Cronkite

CBS newscaster Walter Cronkite blooped the following: "Prayers were offered throughout the world as Pope Paul planned for prostate surgery at the Pentagon . . . that should be the Vatican."

Oh God-Frey

Heard on the Arthur Godfrey morning radio show on CBS: "This is truly a fine product for the relief of aches and pains, so for all of you who find it stiff in the morning, try Bufferin."

All Wet

In one of his traditional introductions of celebrities in his audience Ed Sullivan asked swimming champions Johnny Weismuller and Buster Crabbe to take a bow, after which he told his nationwide audience that ". . . these two fine gentlemen are being put into the Swimming Hole of Fame."

Don't Miss It If You Can

ANNOUNCER: " 'Tuesday Night at the Movies' will be seen on Saturday of this week instead of Monday."

I Love Lucy

DISC JOCKEY: ". . . continuing now with more music from the album *'Mr. Lucy Goes Latin'* . . . that should be *Mr. Lucky* . . . we hear a selection "Coffee Bells and Cow Beans" . . . I mean "Cow Bells and Coffee Beans" as performed by Henry Mancini and his swinging organ."

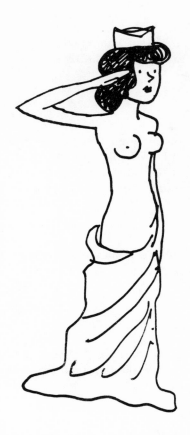

At Ease

QUIZ MASTER: "All right, young lady, before we ask you your first question, what branch of service are you in?

CONTESTANT: I am a Wave.

QUIZ MASTER: My, you must be proud to wear your uniform. Tell me . . . what is the first thing you are taught as a Wave?

CONTESTANT: One of the first things we learned is, before we do anything to disgrace our uniforms, we should take them off."

Picket March

COMMENTATOR: ". . . and as Labor leader George Meany made his way to the speaker's stand the band struck up 'Stars and Strikes Forever.' "

Ready Eddie

NEWSCASTER: "It was reported that Connie Stevens was about to give birth to a child. When questioned, Eddie Fisher would not comment about the impending blessed event. This report was verified by a source believed responsible."

Miss-Take

Heard on Hy Gardner's Miami television program: "It has been erroneously reported that Christine Jorgenson is flat-busted."

Pitch Man

SPORTSCASTER: "Here is a sports bulletin just received from the news room. It is now official! Juan Pizzaro has just pissed a no hit-no run ball game!"

Beauty and the Beast

Johnny Carson had five Miss America contestants as guests on his program, as well as other guests. He referred to them in this fashion: ". . . and on our show tonight we have five Miss America contestants and also some dogs (AUDIENCE ROARS) . . . I mean real dogs (MORE AUDIENCE LAUGHTER) . . . come on, now, you know I mean dogs that bark!"

Hot Stuff

MOVIE COMMERCIAL: " 'Saturday at the Movies' brings you another hit motion picture. See Elizabeth Taylor and Paul Newman together in a *Cot on a Hot Tin Roof.*"

Family Show

Arlene Francis asked a young lady whose occupation was being guessed on "What's My Line" if she worked for a nonprofit organization. Emcee John Daly consulted with her for a moment and then told the panel: "I must warn you that there is a hooker here."

Father of Our Country

STATION BREAK: "Stay tuned for 'Peyton Place,' where today you will meet Dr. Michael Rossi, who is responsible for most of the children born in this small country town."

Yes, We Have No Bananas

WIOD, Miami, disc jockey Tom Gauger tells about the announcer who blooped, "Metropolitan Opera star Anna Moffo will now sing 'The Star-Spangled Banana.'"

Good Night!

"This is Art Linkletter saying good night . . . and a special thanks to you, Edith Head, and your girls for bringing your dresses down on our program."

Break Bread

When Durwood Kirby devoted the CBS "Dimension" radio program to Kermit Schafer's Blooper book entitled *Prize Bloopers,* he recalled the time he announced the opening of a radio program thusly: "The Blonde Bed Breakers are on the air! . . . I mean *The Bond Bread Bakers!*"

Miss Conception

In the 1965 Miss America Beauty Pageant the emcee was back-stage talking to the five semifinalists while the judges were choosing Miss America, when he came up with this Blooper: "Have you ever seen five more expectant young ladies?"

For You, Deefeecult

On Johnny Carson's "The Tonight Show" a collector of butterflies was Johnny's guest. When Johnny was shown some handsome frames that displayed the butterflies under glass, Johnny asked, "How do you mount a butterfly? It must be very difficult."

He's a Big One!

Johnny Carson during a lead-in for a Jolly Green Giant commercial looked into a camera and said, "Have you ever walked out of your house and found yourself face to face with a huge green fruit?"

Red Face

On the "Red Skelton Show" a few years ago Red was talking about root beer; he suggested to his viewers that they drink plenty of root beer because "it is good for your root." It took the audience quite a while to get over that one!!

Air Sick

Frank McGee, NBC News, gave this information to the viewing public during the course of a Gemini space flight: "I have just learned that we do have the film of the astronauts' breakfast, which should be coming up shortly."

Wrong Channel

Disc Jockey: ". . . . and here now is another million seller sung by popular Urethra Franklin . . . *Aretha!*"

Saucy Commercial

"So look for Hunt's tomato sauce on your favorite grocer's can . . . *shelf!*"

Good Deed for the Day

LOCAL NEWS: "The Girl Scouts in this area are planning to
form a Little Mothers Club much like the already formed
Little Fathers Club headed by their scout master. All Girl
Scouts interested in becoming 'little mothers' are to meet
with the Boy Scout Master in the high school gym after this
meeting."

You Only Hurt the One You Love

DISC JOCKEY: "We hear now the horny sound of Al Hirt . . . I mean the horny horn of Al Hirt . . . the horn sound of Al Hirt!!! . . . I'm really sorry, Al."

Without Rhyme or Reasoner

"This is Harry Reasoner reminding you to tune in this Sunday when CBS-TV will prevent the Johnson wedding!"

Elementary, My Dear Watson

NEWSCASTER: "The battered bodies of the two young women, both clad in black bathing suits, were found by fishermen Friday night in a canal off the Intracoastal Waterway, a quarter of a mile north of the Dania Beach Boulevard bridge. The younger girl had been shot fatally and her companion, believed to be Mrs. Frank, was killed from a blow on the back of the head with a sharp object—possibly an ax. Both had fractured skulls from blows on the back of the head, and both of the attractive young women were stabbed in the upper abdomen. Their bodies were tied around the neck with electrical cord to two concrete blocks . . . . Police suspect foul play!"

A Smash

"Here is a bulletin from NBC News . . . Newark, New Jersey . . . Militant Civil Rights leaders, angered by the presence of newsmen at their meeting, smashed cameras and TV equipment . . . and now back to 'Beat The Press' . . . er . . . '*Meet The Press*'!"

A Hot Number

COMMERCIAL: "So stop by our downtown store and visit our fashion center. You will see our lovely models in heat . . . (PAUSE, TURNS PAGE) . . . resistant fabrics which will keep you cooler this summer."

Dead Men Tell No Tales

PUBLIC SERVICE ANNOUNCEMENT: "So when you drive, be sure to keep a safe distance from the car in front of you; tail-getting will get you nowhere . . . that should be tail-gating."

A Nose for News

NEWSCASTER: ". . . and now for some nose newts!"

He Lipths

On the "Mike Douglas Show" Mike was having a discussion with Sheila MacRae and a well-known children's doctor. Mike asked: "Doctor, is it dangerous to thuck your sumb?"

The Story of Peter Pan

COMMERCIAL: ". . . and so, ladies, on your next trip to your grocer be sure to order Peanut Pan Peter Butter."

Sacrilegous Song

ANNOUNCER: ". . . and now our guest soloist, Marian Anderson, will sing Gounod's 'Oyvey Maria.' "

Help!

Curt Gowdy dropped this classic during the broadcast of the AFL All-Star Game. Noting that a downpour had formed a small lagoon on the field of play, he remarked: "If there's a pileup there, they'll have to give some of the players artificial insemination."

I'd Rather Fight

COMMERCIAL: "So be among the many who change over to mild-tasting Phillies cigars. Remember . . . all the fellas are switching to Fellas . . . I mean Phillies."

Local News

"Be sure to attend the Elks' Club Charity Beer Drinking Contest with entry fees going to charity. The beer drinking contest starts Wednesday afternoon with eliminations all day Thursday."

Say It Isn't So!

On "You Don't Say" daytime program the emcee has two lights on the panel in front of him that flash the contestants' score. Once when one of the lights conked out, he looked down and said, "Hey, my little thing isn't working!" The audience roared. After the laughter died down, he looked at guest panelist Vincent Price and said, "Don't you say one word!"

I Wish I Was Single Again

On a David Susskind "Open End" TV program, a birth control authority was his invited guest, who told viewers "that a birth control experiment is soon to start at a single clinic (AUDIENCE TITTERS) . . . by a single clinic, I don't mean for people who are single!"

Oh, Oh

When Art Linkletter interviewed columnist Hedda Hopper on his "Talent Scouts" show, the discussion drifted to old stars of yesteryear. Linkletter asked Hopper how she thought today's crop of actors stacked up against the likes of Douglas Fairbanks, Sr. She replied, "Sean Connery is the closest." Art said, "Oh, you mean 007? . . . Yes, he fixes everybody." Hedda snapped back with: "Yes, and he especially fixes the girls!"

Kentucky Bourbon

SPORTSCASTER: "For western Kentucky, All-American Bobby Rascoe was high with twenty-seven pints!"

Born Yesterday

Virginia Graham, femcee of her "Girl Talk" TV show on NBC, had screen actress Angie Dickinson as her guest, who told of her recently born child. Miss Graham asked, "How old was she when she was born?"

Livid Color

When Lana Turner was a mystery guest on "What's My Line," the question came around to Bennett Cerf. He asked if she was best known as a pin-up girl. Miss Turner said, "No." John Daly interrupted, saying, "Well, actually, that's a broad question." After the audience laughter had subsided, John Daly said, "I thank God we are not in color, I haven't blushed in twenty years!"

Baby Talk

Nancy Dickerson, NBC news commentator, was describing the events surrounding the birth of President Johnson's first grandchild. The TV station accidentally cut off the word *cigars* from her last news item detailing this happy event, with the following result: "Lucy's husband, Pat Nugent, when he learned of the blessed event, passed out . . ."

Duped

Ralph Renick, WTVJ, Miami, news director and commentator, was reaching the end of one of his strongly worded editorials. The subject was waste in government. He paused to let the facts sink in and then said in measured tones, "We must do away with this dupeless needication."

Girl Watchers

NEWSCASTER: "Mayor John Lindsay said he will keep an eye on the topless situation in New York; he further said that the courts will also take a close look at the girls."

Lest We Forget

Maggie McNellis interviewed a famous screen personality on her "Luncheon at the Latin Quarter" program. She told the audience of the great unforgettable motion picture her guest starred in and, for the world of her, couldn't think of what it was about.

She Sells Sea Shells

Former Miss America Bess Meyerson, describing the beauty pageant, told of the bathing beauties spending the day taking pictures on the broad walk at the she shore in Atlantic City.

Fish Story

On the popular TV cooking program "The French Chef," featuring Julia Child, the following was heard: "It's best to go to the fish market early Friday morning and leave your odor."

Give the Girl a Handout

Ed Sullivan, introducing a guest in his audience, blooped the following: "Sitting out in our audience is talented Dolores Gray, currently starving on Broadway."

Order, Please

When Pope Paul visited this country, he stayed at Cardinal Spellman's residence in New York. NBC's Bill Ryan, who described this momentous visit, told the TV millions that "Pope Paul has just left Cardinal Spellman's restaurant . . . . er, residence . . . . after having a bite to eat, for Yankee Stadium."

Curtain Time

On PLAY YOUR HUNCH, starring Merv Griffin as emcee, there were three men shown, to stump the contestants. Each one had a pole in his hand with the upper part obscured by a curtain. On only one of these poles, a mason's hod was balanced. Merv said, "Now to score another point, can you tell me which one of these men has a bog on his pole!"

The Last Roundup

A news director at WORL in Boston started each morning with a twenty-five-minute news roundup. His first story on this particular morning came out, "Police in Danvers this morning discovered the half-nude body of a man lodged in a sewer pipe. Although not believed to be connected to the current rash of gangland slayings, police have termed the death a sewercide."

Bungles for Britain

While in London I was listening to the BBC, and I heard what I thought was a classic blooper on a TV station featuring a dramatic program depicting the Battle of Britain during World War II. I ran for my notebook when I heard the actress say to her soldier boyfriend, "I know everything will be all right, if you will only keep your pecker up." It wasn't until some time later that I discovered that "pecker" meant courage.

Humpty Bumpty

Wire service typos are very often responsible for newscasters' goofs, especially when news is read "cold" right off the ticker. Here is an example of a newsman's reading an Associated Press news item that was handed to him which he was on the air and which was broadcast over KFRB, Alaska. "A secretary who humped her boss caused more than five thousand dollars in damages. . . . Er, I'm sure they must have meant 'Bumped into her boss!' "

Congratulations

On "The Today Show," newsman Lem Tucker told about: "Lynda Bird Robb who had a little baby girl shortly after midwife . . . *midnight!*"

Swan Song

During a coast-to-coast broadcast of the Metropolitan Opera on ABC, Lauritz Melchior, distinguished tenor of the Met, was singing the leading role in *Lohengrin*. In the last act he was supposed to leave the stage in a boat drawn by swans; however, the swans missed the cue of the stage crew and left the stage while Melchior was still singing. In complete calm, he turned to his fellow performers and said: "What time does the next swan leave?"

Watch Your P's and Q's

COMMENTATOR: "Ronald Reagan was expected to make a personal pee to the G.O.Plee Platform Committee."

Doin' What Comes Naturally

On the Johnny Carson show the following situation came up: Johnny was interviewing Helen and Frank Beardsley of California, parents of 20 children. Johnny asked how do you manage, having 20 children? Mrs. Beardsley replied, "I'm doing what I enjoy most, I guess I was just made for it."

The audience went wild. After they left, Johnny said, "I only have three children, I don't know how they do it." Someone from the audience hollered, *"Oh, yes you do!"*

Beat Me, Daddy

WEATHER FORECASTER: "Well, folks, it's raining again . . . and the sun is shining. I've heard it said that when it rains when the sun is out, the Devil is beating his wife. It looks like he's been banging her . . . that is, beating her, all week."

Heaven Can Wait

Seen on Art Linkletter's "House Party": LINKLETTER: "Do you have any pets?" LITTLE GIRL: "No, I did have a fish but he died." LINKLETTER: "And it went to fish heaven?" LITTLE GIRL: "No, I threw him down the toilet."

Frank Question, Frank Answer

A youngster, when being interviewed during intermission in a Montreal-New York Hockey Game, was asked this question by Frank Selky, Jr.:

"Did you have a nice Christmas?"

"No."

"Why?"

"I'm Jewish!"

Having a Ball

Lucille Ball appeared as a guest on the new "Virginia Graham Show." Also appearing as a guest was a magician, who was displaying his remarkable sleight-of-hand tricks with little disappearing balls. At one point of his act he told Lucille, "You think I have two balls," to which she replied, "I hope so!"

Give Him a Hand

A new disc jockey was understandably nervous his first day on the air. His assignment was to "break" a new Beatles record. This was the result: "Here is the next number one record by the Beatles: 'I Want to Hold Your Gland . . . *Hand!'* "

The Birds and the Bees

Singer Pat Boone appeared as a guest cohost on "The Mike Douglas Show." Pat brought with him his wife, Shirley, and his four daughters, who sang on the program. When Mike probed into Pat's married life, he asked if Shirley traveled with him, to which Pat replied, "It seemed that my wife Shirley was always pregnant until we found out what was causing it. . . . I mean—" (The audience laughter continued into the next commercial, and viewers never did find out what he meant.)

A Great Pair

SPECIAL EVENTS: The following blooper occurred when beautiful Raquel Welch was called upon to make an Academy Award presentation: "My name is Raquel Welch. . . . I am here for visual effects" (*Audience laughter*) "And I have two of them. (*More Laughter.*) I mean nominations for *Marooned* and *Krakatoa, East of Java!*"

Aces Wild

A radio station in Seattle, Washington, broadcasts the Super-Sonics basketball games. A sponsor of these games is Richfield Products and Credit Cards. A hapless announcer was expounding on the virtues of the Richfield credit card when this popped out: "Yessiree folks, Richfield credit cards are like an ass in the hole (*Gulp.*) So why don't you keep one up your . . . (*Gulp*) uh . . . sleeve!"

Prune Bowl

ANNOUNCER: "See color cleverage of all the major college bowel games New Year's day on NBC."

Holy Cow!

Herb Rau, Miami news columnist, reported the following, which occurred on a Channel 6, Miami, newscast: "An announcer talked about one of the FBI's most wanted criminals and on the screen, inadvertently, we hope, flashed a picture of Pope Paul."

Double Meaning

Jack Paar, always known for coming out with the unpredictable, introduced movie star Jayne Mansfield thus: "And here they are . . . Jayne Mansfield!"

No Bunk

A hillbilly singer, Cecil Gill, was scheduled to sing, "There's An Empty Cot in the Bunk House Tonight." The announcer fluffed "Cecil Gill, the Yodeling Country Boy, will now sing, 'There's An Empty Bunk in the Cathouse Tonight.' "

Flying High

Larry King, popular radio and TV personality, broadcasting the color during the telecast of the Miami Dolphins–Baltimore Colts football game, observed: "Now coming onto the field to entertain the fans is the Air Force Academy Drug and Bugle Corps."

Age Before Beauty

Bob Hope, sponsor of the annual Desert Classic Golf Tournament from Palm Springs, California, was stalling for time while Arnold Palmer and Ray Floyd were out on the golf course playing, sudden death having come into the eighteenth hole in a tie. This was the tournament in which the celebrated Vice President Spiro T. Agnew "beanings" took place. Hope decided to interview the scantily attired Desert Classic girls who acted as scorekeepers. He asked one girl, "How old are you?" "Twenty-four" she replied. "I've got balls older than that," said Hope. Realizing what he had said when he heard the audience surrounding the eighteenth hole roar, he countered with, "Of course, I mean *golf balls!*"

Help!

PUBLIC SERVICE ANNOUNCEMENT: "And now this tip from the American Red Cross. In case of drowning, lay the girl . . . lay the drowning victim on her back and try mouth-to-mouth breeding . . . (GULP) *breathing!*"

Get Out Of Town

News Director Dave Duncan of WLKW, Rhode Island was the victim of this emergency news bulletin: "From his emergency flood headquarters at City Hall, Mayor Friedman has just ordered all families living near or adjacent to the Mill River to ejaculate immediately."

Flipping His Lid

Accepting the Oscar award in behalf of Cliff Robertson, Academy Award winner for the best actor role in *Charlie,* the recipient said that he regretted that Robertson was not present, "as he was *flipping* in the *Filmapinnes.*"

Peep Show

Singer Roberta Sherwood appeared as a guest on a program starring radio and TV personality Bill Goodwin. The conversation got around to Walter Winchell, who discovered Roberta in a small nightclub in Miami.

BILL: "Walter Winchell was there peeking through keyholes?"

ROBERTA: "He wasn't peeking through keyholes."

BILL: "That his racket. They say he looks through peeholes."

     (*Audience hysteria.*)

Mind Blower

SPONSOR: "I am speaking to you from the National Bowling Championship featuring the nation's top lady blowers . . . bowlers . . . and our next blower is Myrtle Haggarity . . . *bowler!*"

Just Ducky

News director John Nance tells about the time ABC newsman Peter Jennings blooped, "A group of American marines got a good look at how the Vietcong treat their prisoners today in the jungles of South Vietnam. A Marine patrol came across the remains of a small VC prison camp near the jungle highlands village of Fuck Doh . . . that should be Duc Pho."

Out of this World

When Astronaut Wally Schirra appeared as a guest for an interview on "Meet the Press," panelist Lawrence Spivak asked: "How does it feel to be in a state of *wastelessness?*"

47

A Stopper

An attractive and well-stacked young lady came on "The Virginia Graham Show" to do a commercial, as she had previously done on several TV shows. Comic Dennis Wholey, a guest on the program, quipped, "Here she is again . . . the plug of the week!"

Deuces Wild

SPORTSCASTER: "I'm standing at the rear of the green of the short one hundred forty-five yard par three. With the wind behind them, most of the girl pros easily reached this green with a six or a seven iron. In yesterday's round the wind was blowing in the opposite direction; only one girl had a douche on this hole . . . DEUCE!"

By George

On "Name That Tune," emcee George De Witt was desperately trying to give a young lady, who was recently married, the clue to the song title, "I Love You." After she missed the title several times the emcee hinted, "What did you say to your husband on your wedding night?" After a few seconds of thought she replied, "Gosh, that's a hard one."

Billy the Kid

Many of the talk shows have music when it's time for a commercial. David Frost, anticipating just such a moment, observed, "We have to take a break, because I can see Billy is about to tinkle again."

Pay As You Go

COMMERCIAL: "And remember—at People's Credit, you pee whichever way is easiest for you."

Rock Festival

NEWSCASTER: "Good evening. Here are tonight's headlines: 'Nixon Gets Stoned On Trip' . . ."

Honesty is the Best Policy

The TV play was *Abe Lincoln in Illinois* . . . in which Raymond Massey starred. The actors on stage were bidding farewell to the president. . . . When one of them called out . . . "G'bye Mister Massey."

Tongue Twister

NEWSCASTER: "The only way the man could be identified was by the fact that he was standing in the road alongside his stalled automobile with a cool tit in his hand."

Henny Youngman

COMMERCIAL: "Houchens Market has fresh young hens ready for the rooster . . . er . . . roaster."

Falling Stars

Candy Jones, mistress of ceremonies on the TV program YOUR LUCKY STAR on WPIX in New York, told her viewers: "Tonight we are going to find out which Hollywood movie stars were born under the sign of Crappycorn."

Lost in a Fog

WEATHER FORECASTER: "It seems that we haven't had much weather lately . . . for some reason we don't get too much of it this time of year."

Rock and Roll

NEWSCASTER: "Also keeping an eye on the Woodstock Rock Festival was New York's Governor Rockin Nelsenfeller!!!"

Shot-Gun Wedding

On a program entitled "It's Your Move," emanating from Canada, emcee Paul Hanover welcomed back a guest contestant who had missed a few programs as a result of getting married. Hanover innocently asked, "How come you had to go and get married like that?" Her comeback was: "Oh, we didn't *have* to get married!"

Young at Heart

Gig Young appeared as a guest on "The Merv Griffin Show." Gig dwelt on the fact that he is no longer married. Merv innocently asked, "Do you find it hard getting up in the morning since you're a bachelor?"

Get the Picture?

Johnny Carson had Tony Randall as his guest on the "Tonight Show." Johnny asked Tony to read a cue card for his next commercial, Camelon panty hose. Tony read, "and now here's a word about a panty hose that fits almost any man or woman. . . ." While trying to figure that one out, Johnny was holding up a Kodak camera sign. He blurted out, "Now here's a word from Kotex . . . *Kodak.*"

Believe It or Not

The following excerpt is reported verbatim from a live broadcast. The name of the program is "Central Florida Showcase." This question is being asked of Dr. Robert Cade, the inventor of the drink Gatorade: "What did the original drink taste like, doctor?" "The first Gatorade was served to a football team. A player got it. He was a guard at the University who plays with the Steelers now. He got the first drink of Gatorade, took a big swallow, and said, "This stuff tastes like piss!"

Ladies' Day

Hugh Downs had Timothy Leary as his guest on "The Today Show." The discussion centered about Leary's provocative books on habit-forming drugs. Downs interrupted the discussion with, "Before we continue, let's take a look at this type of pot that the ladies will enjoy—*TEFLON!*"

Chick and Double Chick

A television network news commentator, describing the historic Apollo moon landing, observed that "Astronaut Alan Shepard is now going over his chick list before launching."

Hard Question

Heard on the ABC-TV "Newlywed Game." "Couple number three: What Beatle song reminds you of your wedding night?" "It's Been a Hard Day's Night!"

London Fog

When I was in London, I watched TV personality Simon Dee on London's ITV network. Simon Dee conducts a nighttime TV program very similar to Johnny Carson's, Merv Griffin's, and Dick Cavett's in the States. Simon had as his guest Millicent Martin, a popular singer in England. She explained that she was quite nervous that night because her husband, a producer, had a show opening titled, *"Vivat! Vivat! Vagina!. . . .* I mean *Vivat! Vivat! Regina!"*

Dumb Bunny

SPORTSCASTER: Many different kinds of animals have interrupted football games, but perhaps none so unusual as this one: "It's a big hippity-hop rabbit, jacking off down the field."

Of Mice and Men

SPORTSCASTER: "This is Jack Drees bringing you another major PGA Tournament from the White Mouse Country Club in Philadeplhia . . . I'm sorry, that should be White Marsh Country Club."

Small Talk

DISC JOCKEY: "COCM Stereo Land now presents popular Hawaiian favorite Don Ho with Tiny Boobies . . . uh . . . Tiny Bubbles"

My Old Kentucky Home

COMMERCIAL: "So folks, if you are looking for the easy way to enjoy your dinner this Sunday, just drop by the colonel's place for delicious finger lickin' Kenfucky fried chicken."

Is This Any Way to Run an Airline?

When "Playhouse Ninety" was telecast live over the CBS network several years ago, a drama in which a passenger airplane had lost one motor was the theme. The actress portraying a stewardess came up with this line in the excitement of the moment: "Will all passengers pease deplene from the real exit . . . er . . . er . . . will all passengers please pee out the real exit. . . . Thank you."

Can't Believe I Ate . . .

An early-morning DJ did his first commercial. All went well until he tried getting beyond the following portion from the copy department: "You will love this delicious bread. By the way, did you know how the sandwich got its name? The Earl of Sandwich was the first man to put his meat between two pieces of bread."

Food for Thought

Graham Kerr, the emcee of his own delightful cooking show, "The Galloping Gourmet," came up with this classic when he was talking about squid: "A squid, as you know of course, has ten testicles . . . ten *tentacles*. Oh, my gosh!"

Fall Guy

Radio and television interviewers often have difficulty keeping their programs interesting and brisk. Some will very often think ahead to their next question before actually hearing the answer to their previous question, as evidence a portion of this interview:

INTERVIEWER: "Tell us about your recent safari to Africa."

GUEST: "I am sorry to tell you that this particular trip you refer to was canceled when I slipped in my bathroom and suffered a severe brain concussion, and as a result I was hospitalized for eight weeks."

INTERVIEWER: "Really? . . . How wonderful . . . What about your trip to the Congo?"

Watch It!

John Cameron Swayze, veteran newscaster who has become identified with the Timex commercials and their underwater demonstrations, was telling about one of his sponsor's new watches in this fashion. "So when you are in the market for a perfect gift, may we *rewind* you about Timex."

Thanks a Lot

NEWSCAST: "This is DIMENSION, Allen Jackson reporting on the CBS Radio Network from New York. Today's big news story is the national spreading of the flu epidemic . . . brought to you by the Mennen Company!"

To the Rear, March!

ANNOUNCER: "And now the band will pay a tribute to the rear of Senator Barry Goldwater!!"

Asleep in the Deep

WEATHER FORECASTER: "The six A.M. forecast is for partly croudy with a seventy-five percent chance of rain mixed with sleep early this morning."

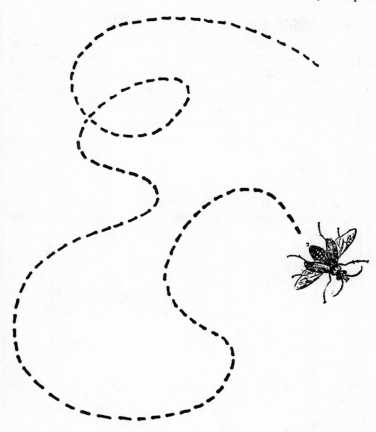

Fly Now, Play Later

Dan Rowan of "Laugh In" appeared with Dick Cavett on
his late night program. Rowan seemed to be bothered by a
fly during the course of his interview. Dick kept kidding him
about the pest, and at one point he said, "After station break,
we'll talk about your fly."

55

While Burns Roams

On the Johnny Carson TONIGHT SHOW, George Burns told Rosemary Clooney that after 38 years, singing is all he can do. He then asked Rosemary . . . "How come you and José Ferrer have five children?" to which she replied "José doesn't sing!" "Oh, he does it the hard way," Burns snapped back.

To the Rear

Faye Emerson, on the Arthur Godfrey TV program, bloopered the following: "Walter Slezak, whenever I think of you, I think of your Fanny . . . Of course I mean your starring role in *Fanny!*"

Double Trouble

QUIZ EMCEE: "All right now, for a twenty-five-dollar savings bond, you have fifteen seconds to name as many things as you can that come in pairs."

CONTESTANT: "Let's see . . . shoes . . . gloves . . . er, *brassieres!*"

Special Elections

COMMENTATOR: "And from France comes word that action will not be taken on this important matter until after their general erections!"

Just Peachy

David Brinkley, during the description of former Congresswoman Rankin's unprecedented protest trip to Washington, told his viewers that ". . . accompanying Miss Rankin are 5,000 women peach marchers."

Simple Arithmetic

On an interview program conducted by Johnny Olsen, a young lady was asked her age. She made it a point to emphasize that she was twenty-one years old. When she was asked what she was doing in New York, she replied, "Oh, I'm here with my parents . . . they are celebrating their twentieth anniversary today."

Good Show

On ABC's WIDE WORLD OF SPORTS, emcee Jim McKay was describing the World Barrel-Jumping Championship, and came out with this classic. "Leo Lebel has been competing with a pulled stomach muscle, showing a lot of guts!"

Johnny on the Spot

In the televised description of an important PGA golf tournament, the following was heard: "And now Johnny Tee is on the pot . . . of course I mean John Pott is on the tee!"

When You Gotta Go

POLITICAL RALLY: "And now, moments before the polling of the delegates officially starts, I see Representative West making his way to the rest room . . . I beg your pardon . . . Representative West is making his way to the rostrum!!!"

Nuts to You

COOKING PROGRAM: "Good morning. Today we are going to bake a spice cake, with special emphasis on *how to flour your nuts!*"

Him Tarzan

Art Linkletter asked a little girl whom she would choose if she could have two movie stars as parents for a day. Her reply was Art and Zsa Zsa Gabor . . . because Zsa Zsa sounded like an African name, and Art would make a good Tarzan. Art, not thinking, said, "I can't wait to swing from limb to limb. . . . Uh, I mean from tree to tree!"

Off Key

ANNOUNCER: "Excuse me, Senator . . . I am sure that our listening audience would like to hear more about the fine work that your important Congressional committee is doing . . . but unfortunately, Margaret Truman is about to sing."

We Don't Mean United Press

SPOT ANNOUNCEMENT: "This is KLZ-TV, Denver . . . . When you are thirsty, try 7-UP, the refreshing drink in the green bottle with the big 7 on it and *U-P* after!"

Hold That Line

SPORTSCASTER: "Do you find the Chicago Bears have very complicated plays?"
COACH: "I've talked to some defensive players, and they are all pretty simple!"

You're Getting to be a Habit With Me

On the Jack Paar TONIGHT SHOW, Eva Gabor, wanting to tell Paar that she watched his show every night, came out with this classic. "You know, Jack, I go to sleep with you every night!"

This Must be the Place

COMMERCIAL: "This special offer is good for tomorrow only, and the sale will take place at our wholesale whorehouse . . . I beg your pardon . . . the sale will take place at our wholesale warehouse!!!"

Don't Call Me, I'll Call You

This occurred on a television dramatic presentation during the Christmas season. During a scene in which a group of carolers was singing, an actor was supposed to go up to a friend of his who was a member of the group, and greet him warmly with, "George, yah ol' buzzard, ah ain't seen yah in a long time." However, what came out was this, much to the chagrin of all. "George, yah ol' bastard, ah ain't seen yah in a long time." P.S. The actor ain't been around in a long time.

One Track Mind

On the Steve Allen late-night program, Steve interviewed an authority on health:

STEVE ALLEN: "What is your suggestion for a healthy way to start the day?"

GUEST: "First thing in the morning, drink five gallons of water.

STEVE ALLEN: "And then?"

GUEST: "Then you go to the bathroom."

STEVE ALLEN: "What kind of breakfast would you recommend?"

GUEST: "First you go to the bathroom."

STEVE ALLEN: "Please . . . I'm asking about breakfast."

GUEST: "First you go to the bathroom."

STEVE ALLEN: (HYSTERICALLY): "The bathroom . . . the bathroom . . . I mean the breakfast . . . the breakfast!!!"

Ace Is Wild

NEWSCASTER: "Also in attendance was former Governor Joe Foss, famed flying ass of World War II."

On the Button

COMMERCIAL: "So, cold sufferers, stop at your drug store first thing tomorrow and pick up a bottle of Vicks Naval Spray!"

Junior Announcer

Steve Allen recalls the time when he was an announcer in Phoenix, Arizona, and a fellow announcer introduced a news program in this fashion: "Stay tuned for Fulton Lewis and the Jews . . . I mean Fulton Lewis, Jr., and the news . . . and now Mr. Junior!"

Crack the Whip

TV WANT ADS: ". . . and anyone who qualifies for any of these jobs can phone our station. Today we are looking for someone to fill a spot as an efficient *sadistical* secretary . . . with no bad habits and who is willing to learn."

Sonny Tufts? ? ?

Sonny Tufts, who has been the butt of many a good-natured kidding, was being interviewed on radio. He blooped, "I don't give a goddamn what newspaper people write about me . . . (PAUSE) . . . I'm awfully sorry about my language . . . really, I'm goddamned sorry!"

A Beaut

During the course of the Miss America Pageant choosing the 1968 beauty queen, Bert Park's microphone went dead just as he was to sing the pageant's traditional theme song "There She Goes, Miss America."

A dutiful announcer on a station carrying the network special told viewers: "Bert Parks' singing is not the fault of your local station . . . it's due to network audio problems during the crowing . . . I mean *crowning* of 'Miss America.' As soon as difficulties are restored, we will hear him sing."

Kooks

The following blooper occurred on an evening network news program: "For the latest report on racial strife in the South, we switch you to our reporter in Montgomery, Alabama." "After a night of tension here in Alabama caused by burnings attributed to members of the Ku Ku Lux Kan . . . Klu Klutz Klan . . . the Que Que Klux Klan . . . (*in exasperation*) *the KKK! . . .*"

Everybody Loves Somebody Sometime

When Dean Martin and Jerry Lewis were teamed together they made a motion picture for Paramount entitled *The Caddy*. They made several spot commercials, plugging the picture. This is how one of the printable takes went: "Hello, everybody, this is Dean Martin." "And this is Jerry Lewis, telling you to see our latest picture for Paramount called *The Caddy*." Dean went on to say, "*The Caddy* is one of the most righteous pictures you will ever see—" Jerry interrupted, "Righteous? Where the fuck do you see 'Righteous?' That's riotous, you greaseball!"

False Impressions

Eva Gabor appeared as a guest on "The Merv Griffin Show." Merv asked if she was afraid of being robbed after appearing on the program with her sparkling necklace being shown on the camera. Merv kept looking at her necklace, which draped her low-cut gown. She replied, "You know, Merv, everything I got is fake. . . . I mean jewelry!"

Fly-By-Night

TV personality Hugh Downs relates the story about movie actor Adolphe Menjou, for years one of America's Ten Best-Dressed Men, who appeared as a guest on the original Jack Paar "Tonight Show." Mr. Menjou, the epitome of fashion, was told by the unpredictable Paar, "Mr. Menjou, you have failed to activate your zipper!"

From Out of the Blue

Guests on an interview show were discussing the 1969 Academy Awards. A film clip from *Butch Cassidy and the Sundance Kid* was shown in which Butch and Sundance jumped over a cliff uttering a four-letter word. One of the interviewees had commented that this objectionable word was censored. Another guest replied, "Yes, they cut the shit out of *Butch Cassidy*."

Small Wonder

Dr. David Reuben, whose sex book has been a best-seller, appeared as a guest on the Johnny Carson "Tonight" program. He tried to make a point by saying that in this space age we can send an astronaut two hundred ninety-three thousand miles, but he can't get within seven inches of his target. Before he could explain his thought, actor Tony Randall, also a guest, chimed in with, "What's this about an undersized astronaut?"

Knots to You

When I appeared with David Frost as his guest on his TV program, he related this blooper which occurred on the BBC in England. An actor in a dramatic moment was supposed to have said, "Truss the victim up in my tie." However, in the excitement of the action he blooped, "Tie the victim up in my truss."

Look Before You Leak

The following occurred on the NBC-TV panel show called "You're Putting Me On." The situation called for comedian Orson Bean to supply clues to comedienne Peggy Cass so that she might guess the unknown word, "leak."
ORSON: "What have you got when you need a plumber?"
PEGGY: "A flood."
ORSON: "From a faucet?"
PEGGY: "A drip."
ORSON (*in exasperation*): "When you gotta go, you gotta go."
PEGGY: "A leak."

Dead or Alive

"The Ed Sullivan Show" originally was titled "Toast of the Town." At the end of one of Ed's Sunday night programs, the announcer closing the show told the network of viewers that "Ed Sullivan came to you *alive* from CBS in New York."

Promises, Promises

Sportscaster Al DiRogadus, doing a pregame warm-up before the championship Oakland Raider–Kansas City Chiefs football game blooped the following "Today we are going to see a sensational football dame! GAME!"

Below the Belt

Joe Garagiola, emceeing the audience-participation program "He Said–She Said," quizzed celebrity contestant Hugh Downs. The format called for the celebrity's wife to appear on camera. The questions and answers went like this:

JOE: "What was your first impression of your wife?"

HUGH: "Immoral."

JOE: "How come?"

HUGH: "I was hit on the knee by a golf ball and she said it was a good thing it wasn't any higher. She meant *harder!*"

Fair Game

There is no way a TV football fan can completely ignore a Cleveland player named Fair Hooker. ABC-TV tried, and the commentary team of Keith Jackson, Howard Cosell, and former Dallas Cowboy Don Meredith did their best to play it cool during the course of a New York Jets and Cleveland Browns game. But it was mischievous Don, finally defying all Madison Avenue taboos, who nonchalantly observed, "Isn't Fair Hooker a great name?"

Try Geritol

NEWSCASTER: "In Washington, the Senate is discussing giving funds to aid in reasearch for the new Super-Tonic Transport . . . er Super Sonic Transport!"

Simon Says

DISC JOCKEY: ". . . and now we hear selections from the latest Simon and Garfuckel release. . . . Take it away, Simon and Garfunkel!"

Eeny, Meeny, Miny, Mo

On a man-on-the-street interview program, passers-by were asked their opinions of the various provocative skirt lengths. The interrogator directed his mike at the first female he saw, and this was the result. "I have a street walker over here. (*Apologetically*) I'm sorry, madam. I didn't mean it that way. (*Flustered*) Do you prefer the mindee, meenie, or moxie?"

Honesty Is the Best Policy

On "Let's Make a Deal," popular audience participation program, emcee Monty Hall asked a lady in the "Nondealing" area of the audience the question that he regularly asks the entire audience. "And what happens every Saturday night at seven-thirty." Instead of the usual answer, "Let's Make a Deal," she cracked up the audience with, "I take a bath."

Play Ball!

While watching a Cleveland Indians–Oakland Athletics baseball game, Bob Neal (Cleveland announcer) noticed that owner Charlie O. Finley had come up with another gimmick at his ball park. He had put ball girls along the foul lines instead of ball boys. Mr. Neal blooped, "It appears that Mr. Finley has decided to let girls chase the boys' balls instead of boys chasing boys' . . . *boys' chasing balls!*"

A Nose for News

NEWSCASTER: "Again—Scotch Soup covers the nose."

Wild Announcer

STATION PROMOTION: "See Jack Paar's wildlife on NBC. That is, his wildlife TV special on lions on NBC."

Take Me Out to the Ball Game

During one of the lulls at a Minnesota Twins baseball game, the camera took some close-ups of the fans in the stands. The sportscaster observed two young neckers seated behind third base. He innocently remarked, "Ha, there's two lovers in the stands. He kisses her on the strikes, and she kisses him on the balls."

Hard of Hearing

Heard on "The Newlywed Game," ABC's popular audience-participation program:
EMCEE: "Now, wives, how would you describe your mattress on your honeymoon—soft, medium, or hard?"
WIFE: "Was that before or after we were married?"

Soap in Mouth

SOAP OPERA: "Dad, when Mary told me that she was going to leave me after all these years, and was taking the children with her . . . well, I was just flabberbastard . . . er . . . a faggerbastard . . . *flaggergasted!*"

Order, Please

During a "live" telecast of the KRAFT THEATRE, the dramatic excitement of the most suspenseful moment of the play was reached when above the actors' voices was heard, *"Who ordered the ham on rye?"* The luncheonette delivery boy had walked right into the studio unobserved.

He Floored 'Em

Tex Antoine, who is known for his Uncle Weathbee fore-caster character on NBC-TV, accidentally dropped his crayon on the floor while doing his nightly weather forecast. He picked it up and told his listeners that "tomorrow's *floorcast* is for cloudy weather."

Little Boy Lost

An announcer broadcasting a Pittsburgh Pirate baseball game on radio described a pop fly that was hit in the direction of the Pirates' five-foot-five shortstop, Clem Kosherek. As the lit-tle infielder disappeared from view behind third base, the sportscaster came out with . . . "Where the hell did Kosherek go?"

Playing in the Cracks

ANNOUNCER: "And now, Van Cliburn playing Tchaikovsky's *Piano Concerto Number One* in Blee Fat Minor . . . I beg your pardon, that should be Fee Blat Minor!!!"

False Start

ANNOUNCER: "Our next selection to be sung by our great bari-tone soloist is Rachmaninoff's 'Oh, Cease Thy Sinning, Maidenform.' . . . That should be, 'Oh, Cease Thy Sinning, Maiden Fair.' (Off mike) Oh, great, Maidenform is a bra!"

Sir?

LOWELL THOMAS: "This report is credited to the president of the British Broad of Trade, Sir Stifford Crapps. . . . Cripps!"

Ladies' Day

A women's amateur golf tournament which was played on
three separate eighteen-hole golf courses, was climaxed by the
presentation of the trophy by the local mayor. He appeared
before the microphone with the winner and said, "It gives
me great pleasure to present this magnificent trophy to Helen
Douglas, the new State Intercourse Champion!!"

71

You Can't Win 'em All
STATION PROMOTION: "Hear latest erection results with David Dick on CBS."

Wrong Turn
Dick Cavett was discussing transsexuals with a medical authority on his late night show. Cavett remarked, "You know, doctor, with all of this confusion about which sex is which, you don't know which way to turn."

Praiseworthy
In the dictionary you will find a word spelled P-A-E-A-N and pronounced pe'an. It means to praise. However, an ice-cream sponsor didn't endorse this announcer's choice of words. "And now is a good time to paean Brody's ice cream."

Hey, Man
Sportscaster Curt Gowdy told football fans that "Tim Brown is back deep to receive the punt, while Jerry Logan's uptight."

Broad Statement
Interviewer Phil Donahue had eminent psychologist Harold Greenwald as his guest. Greenwald appeared in connection with his book entitled *The Elegant Prostitute*. Donahue observed that "after visiting with hundreds of prostitutes, Greenwald has come up with a detailed *broad* study of this problem."

Paging Spiro Agnew
Frank Blair, veteran news man on "The Today Show," advised his viewers that NBC will *prevent* TV coverage of the peace demonstrations from Washington.

No Strings Attached

On the TONIGHT SHOW, host Johnny Carson introduced guest star Shari Lewis in this fashion: "And now a girl who is one of the bust pepiteers in the business!!!"

Foot In Mouth

Jinx Falkenberg, the popular female television star, got herself into this amusing tangle.

"I know that I was asked to accept this award for Senator Kefauver as a housewife, because I think that that's what Senator Kefauver did more than anything else—he brought the Senate Crime Investigating Committee into the home, into the kitchen, and gave us all an idea of what was happening in New York City. I know that luckily I was sick the first days of the hearing, so I spent three days in bed enjoying Rudy Halley.

(AUDIENCE LAUGHTER)

"And I must say, I, I, got to know his every move so very well.

(AUDIENCE LAUGHTER)

"No, what I meant . . .

(AUDIENCE LAUGHTER)

"To say is that I missed . . .

(AUDIENCE LAUGHTER)

"I really, you know what I mean."

A Royal Celebration

At the launching of a ship in Norway, a local announcer, with a fine Oxford accent but not too good a grasp of English, was doing the short-wave broadcast when this occurred:

"The Duchess handled the launching beautifully, smashing the champagne bottle against the prow with the aplomb of an expert. The crowd cheered as she majestically slid down the greasy runway into the sea!"

It Was a Great Fight, Ma

Chet Huntley told his viewers during a Gemini live telecast that the Glenn *fight* was witnessed by the largest audience in history.

Dennis the Menace

TELETHON: "This is Dennis James again. I am glad to report that our total has reached a new high. This is due in part to the many *great neckers* at home who have been staying up late watching our program . . . I mean those who live in Great Neck, Long Island!"

Line Forms to the Right

We take you now to Minneapolis to hear the emcee of a program known as POLKA DANCE PARTY.

"Vell, radio audience, dis is a sad day for dis program. Alice Dale, who has been mistress of ceremonies on this show with me, is leafing after fife years. Ve're going to be sorry to see her go. Da producers of dis program and da sponsors have decided that her replacement will come from the ranks of our loyal radio listeners. All you talented young ladies who feel that you can do da job can apply. So ladies, if you want to be my mistress, call Newton 2-0161."

When You Gotta Go

Children on audience-participation programs are often unpredictable. Let's listen to a kid show of a few years ago known as MAKE A WISH.

EMCEE: "Now Marian, if you had your wish, what would you want most?"

CHILD: "I want to go to the toilet!"

Bodies by Fisher

Ham Fisher, celebrated cartoonist, was a guest judge on the TV beauty contest series to select "Miss New York Television." Ted Steele, popular TV personality, was the emcee, and it was always his custom to conduct a brief interview with the judges. Steele asked Fisher how he liked the girls. Fisher fluffed, "With all the feminine pulchritude around the studio, you have to grasp for breast, I mean gasp for breath."

Out at the Plate

Joe Bolton, WPIX Weatherman, formerly a baseball sportscaster, once lost a job as a result of his excitement during a Newark Bears' ball game, when Ernie Koy hit a home run and Bolton exclaimed, "Jesus Christ! It's over the wall!"

There's a Small Hotel

An emcee on a quiz program asked, "Are there any honeymooners in the audience?" He got one blushing couple whom he then asked, "Well, what are you doing here, and where are you from?" They answered, "Minnesota." "Are you staying in Los Angeles for a while?" "Yes." "At a hotel?" "Oh, no," replied the bridegroom, "we have relations in the Valley!!!"

A Bad Spell of Weather

WEATHER MAN: "The typhoon that hit China caused devastation everywhere. The mainland has been badly battered in the wake of this disaster.' . . . The Chinese people are beginning to dig out with the clearing skies. The weather forecast for that area is for flair and coolie."

People . . . People Who Need People. . . .

DISK JOCKEY: "And now, rock 'n rollers, for the number one record, taking the nation by storm, 'Purple Peter Eaters,' by Sheb Wolley."

Rags to Riches

A young lady on a children's program while relating the story of Cinderella, came up with the following:
"Suddenly Cinderella looked up at the clock—it was striking twelve. . . . As she ran from the palace, she dropped her slipper, but when she reached the door she was again in rags, as the wee-bitching hour struck!"

In the Groove

On smaller radio stations throughout the country, the announcer often doubles as engineer, announcer, producer, director. Let's hear the result of this one man's decision to drop the needle on a transcription, and depart from the studio, for a fifteen-minute break for a cup of coffee. "Remember friends, this is the big holiday weekend coming up, so don't be caught short by unexpected guests. Go to your A and P (NEEDLE STUCK) and P and P and P and P and P. . . ."

Some Yolk

Heard on the Bea Wain–Andre Baruch husband-and-wife radio program.

HUSBAND: "The hen that laid double-yolk eggs will be exhibited at the New York State Fair. However, due to the excessive heat, the hen hasn't laid since last Monday."

WIFE: "This could happen to any of us."

That's the Ticket

In a television dramatic play, an actor portrayed the part of a gangster who had just held up a warehouse. He hurriedly ran to a ticket window in a railroad station to ask the ticket agent for two tickets to Pittsburgh.

"Is this the Allegheny window? Come on, sister, get off the phone. I'm in a hurry, I need two pickets to Tittsburgh!"

Ladies' Home Companion

DISK JOCKEY: "This is Martin Block spinning another record. . . . This time, let's hear from the Mills Brothers, singing 'Be My Wife's Companion'! . . . I beg your pardon . . . that should be, 'Be My Life's Companion.' "

Really Big Star

DISK JOCKEY: "Well, rock 'n rollers, it's time for our mystery-guest contest. If you guess the name of our next artist, our sponsors will send you two tickets to the RKO theatre in your neighborhood. Now the clue to this singer, and this is the only clue I'm going to give you, is that she has two of the *biggest hits* in the country."

Take a Number

DISK JOCKEY: "Before we spin our next Sinatra record, let me tell you about Frank's latest marriage to Mia Farrow. Frank has had three or four wives . . . I'm not sure which one he's on now!"

Many a True Word Is Said In Jest

On I'VE GOT A SECRET, Garry Moore and Wally Cox were putting together some furniture while the blindfolded panel tried to guess what they were doing. In a corner of the studio, a lady was putting together drawers to go in a chest. Time ran out, whereupon Wally Cox commented, "I'm so sorry we didn't get to your drawers." "So am I," replied the lady.

Honesty Is Best Policy

Heard on "Girl Talk" television program, presided over by Virginia Graham: "Once you put down one of her books, you can't pick it up again."

Iron Curtain

NEWSMAN: "And late word from Camp David, President Eisenhower's Maryland retreat, advises that the President and Premier Khrushchev held a private meeting; however, we have no details as to what went on, as newsmen were bored from the conference!"

79

Party Line

Here is the result of NBC's MONITOR program getting its wires crossed with an announcement of a sermon by Billy Graham.

"Princess Marcella Borghese is visiting MONITOR, to tell us about her life as a Princess and a successful businesswoman. The business angle might not be as romantic as you would imagine, But the princess does (CUT IN) Each Night, In The Open Air, Just Behind The New Multi-Million-Dollar Gymnasium."

Nothing Serious, I Hope

Here's a news item that was handed to a newscaster without being checked in advance.

"In the head-on collision of the two passenger cars, five people were killed in the crash, two seriously."

Medicine Man

Hugh Downs, veteran announcer, was doing a Rem Cough Medicine commercial on the JACK PAAR SHOW. He blooped the following. "So when you have a cough due to a cold, always keep some *Rum* on hand!" He countered with, "This may be good cough medicine, but I don't think it was what the sponsor had in mind."

Alice in Blunderland

Durwood Kirby, on Allen Funt's CANDID CAMERA, came out with this candid blooper. "And now back to Alice Funt!"

Talk Is Cheap

Heard on radio station CHTM, Manitoba, Canada: The announcer was commenting on the President and stated: "Richard M. Nixon was today sworn in by *Cheap* Justice Earl Warren."

Author, Author

On an audience-participation program, a woman wrestled with the difficult pronounciation of "Alexandre Dumas." She should have left well enough alone.

ANNOUNCER: "Here's your question. There was a famous French author, who wrote many, many famous stories. He is the man who wrote 'The Black Tulip' and 'The Three Musketeers.' What is the name of this famous French author?"

CONTESTANT: "Oh golly . . . I'm nervous . . . let me see . . . OH! Alexandre Dumb-ass! (LAUGHTER) OH! Henry Dumb-ass!"

A Sleeper

Audience-participation programs give sponsors and networks many a headache due to the unexpected and unplanned remarks by the participants, as evidenced by this nationwide broadcast.

EMCEE: "Oh my, sixteen children! Is your husband in the audience?"

CONTESTANT: "Yes."

EMCEE: "Well, let's call him up on the stage. Let's have a nice round of applause for the father of sixteen children. (APPLAUSE) Sir, where did you spend your honeymoon?"

HUSBAND: "Niagara Falls."

EMCEE: "How long were you there?"

HUSBAND: "Eleven days."

EMCEE: "My oh my, you must have seen and done a lot. How did you spend your time?"

HUSBAND: "In bed."

Parlor Game

ANNOUNCERS *"We will return to our LATE SHOW after a brief massage from our sponsor."*

Out of the Mouths of Babes

EMCEE: "How old are you little boy?"
BOY: "Five years old."
EMCEE: "What does your father do?"
BOY: "He works at Tarbide and Tarbon Company (Carbide and Carbon Chemical Company).
EMCEE: "What do they make there?"
BOY: "Light bulbs and toilet paper."
EMCEE: "What makes you think that?"
BOY: "That's what daddy always brings home in his lunch bucket!"

Bringing Up the Rear

On I'VE GOT A SECRET, actress Betsy Palmer took her turn questioning two mayors and two policemen who happened to be standing behind her.
She blooped, "Does your secret have anything to do with the officers behind?"

Inside Joke

When a station was suddenly cut off the air, the announcer, remembering past instances, dutifully switched on the dead mike and said, "Ladies and gentlemen, due to difficulties beyond our control, we are off the air."

Off Course

NEWSCASTER: "And from the latest report it appears that work is progressing rapidly at the famed intercourse canal! . . . That should be, intercoastal canal."

Candid Cameron

CAMEL'S NEWS REEL *had a mix-up due to an AT&T switching error, when John Cameron Swayze said, "And now to Roy Neal in Philadelphia." Roy Neal's voice came on, but the picture was of a Washington correspondent, sitting back in a swivel chair, his heels on a desk, reading a newspaper. Suddenly a voice cut in, "Good grief, we've got Washington!"*

Forks and Spoonerisms

STATION BREAK: "This is WCAR Detroit. Before or after the theatre, be sure to drop in at the Palm Gardens Restaurant for a pretail cockmeal."

Time to Retire

An announcer picked up a script one day and read it on the air, exactly as it was handed to him. It was a Bulova commercial, the standard time signal, with some additions to be made at appropriate times. Here is what the listener heard: "It's 8 P.M. Bulova Watch Time. On Christmas, say Merry Christmas, and on New Year's, say Happy New Year."

He's Got Poisonality

TONY CANZONERI appeared as a panelist on the Rube Goldberg TV show. The program featured cartoon charades, and panelists were supposed to guess sayings, book titles, movie titles, etc., as they were drawn by Goldberg. Tony, arriving late, was given an answer in advance, to keep his average answers respectable. He was told that the correct answer to one of the charades was "poison ivy." Much to the embarrassment of everyone, he answered "poison ivy" to the first question, the answer to which happened to be Henry Wadsworth Longfellow. He raised his hand and answered "poison ivy" to the second cartoon charade. The answer to this was King Philip III. And so on and on for eight questions, he answered "poison ivy!" The ninth cartoon showed a bottle of poison, and ivy growing on the side of a building. Poor Tony figured it was time to stop answering.

Frank-ly Speaking

WHAT'S MY LINE?, the forerunner and brightest of all TV panel programs, had an anxious moment when Ava Gardner appeared as a mystery guest. Her identity was supposed to be guessed by the blindfolded panelists. Her appearance came at a time when she was having marital difficulties with Frank Sinatra. The panelists began shooting their usual questions at the mystery guest, and all was going well until the question "Are you married?" was asked. Ava said, "Yes." The next question was "Are you glad?" At this point, Stopette, the sponsor, paid for a full minute of silence.

Blues in the Night

DISK JOCKEY: "To continue on with the music of the NIGHT TRAIN SHOW, we dig into the past to bring out an old blues standard, 'I've Got a Crush On You.' And here to sing it, The Queen of the Booze . . . Miss Dinah Washington!"

Let's Go to the Movies Instead

ANNOUNCER: "Tune in on Monday to find out if Perry Mason solves this baffling mystery. I'm sorry, on Monday the program will not be on, due to a special broadcast. Tune in on Tuesday. I'm sorry, on Tuesday the program is going to be pre-empted by a speech by Secretary Dulles. Tune in on Wednesday—no, you'd better consult your papers for the correct time, and when you find out, please let me know!"

Scoring With the Girl

SPORTSCASTER: *"Montreal hockey fans will be happy to learn that their star goalie made his first girl in the last few minutes of play."*

Cut Him Off!

A newscaster was carried away by the excitement of the Cuban invasion. He tried to tell his radio audience about the mobilization of anti-Castro forces.

"Consensus of newsmen's opinions in Havana and Miami is that the people of Cuba are beginning to join antro-Castrate forces . . . anti-Castrate forces!"

Remember the Al and Moe

ANNOUNCER: "You will find Manischewitz wine just right for the holidays, tangy and delicious. This fine wine is also good for any occasion, so remember the Maine, Manischewitz . . . name Manischewitz!"

High Infidelity

MUSIC COMMENTATOR: "Be with us again next Saturday at 10:00 P.M. for the program titled HIGH FIDELITY—a program designed to help music lovers increase their reproduction!"

Hair Bob

Comedian Bob Hope told his radio audience, "Women are wearing bathing suits so short this year that they'll have to get two haircuts."

X Marks the Spot

NEWSCASTER: "Police are now swarming to the scene from all over the county. . . . First reports have it that numerous articles of her clothing were torn and scattered about the scene, and there was evidence of teeth marks on both her . . . (PAUSE) . . . well, that is . . . there were teeth marks on different parts of her body."

Buck Buck Bucket

HILLBILLY DISK JOCKEY: "And now, Zeke Parker sings 'My Hole Has a Bucket In It.' . . . Sorry . . . wrong number . . . that should be, 'My Bucket Has A Hole In It'.—That's quite a difference!"

Sock It To Him!

Sportscaster Chris Schenkel blooped, "The forward pass was caught by a New York Giant receiver . . . with an excellent maneuver he got by a Washington defender . . . he faked him right out of his jocks! . . . (PAUSE) . . . and his shoes as well!"

Hot Off the Griddle

Bill Cullen, master of ceremonies of THE PRICE IS RIGHT, was reading the list of prizes being given away on the program. He said, "And to help you with your cooking, we are giving away an assortment of electrical saucepans, frying pans, etc., and a dutch oven with a *girdle* . . . er, I mean, griddle."

Busman's Holiday

COMMERCIAL: "Remember . . . if you are going a'partying on New Year's Eve, it might be easier and wiser to take the bus than to drive after imbibing. . . . So remember, 'Go by bus and leave the drinking to us!' "

Double Your Pleasure

Johnny Carson, a master of the ad lib, interviewed a couple on his WHO DO YOU TRUST? program.

CARSON: "Do you have any children?"

MAN: "Yes, we have twins, 3½ years old."

CARSON: "That's about the greatest labor-saving device in the world!"

Mental Lapse

NEWSCASTER: "After her apprehension by local authorities, Miss Ellen Benson was confined to a menstrual institution for an indefinite period."

What's Good for the Goose

NEWSCASTER: "Former Vice President Nixon's campaign for Governor of California got a goose today from former President Eisenhower. . . . that should read, got a boost today . . . I'm terribly sorry."

Record on the Bum

ANNOUNCER: "And now we are going to hear a recording of Rimski-Korsakov's 'Bum of the Flightful Bee.' "

Unisex

"Today I would like to explain to all you boys and girls how to go about forming your own 4-H club. The chief requisite is to have an adult leader, like myself, which can be a man or woman or a combination of both."

Queen for a Day

EMCEE: "Well, Mrs. Conklin, you have fifteen seconds in which to answer the question. A correct answer is worth a toaster, a waffle iron, a mixer and an eight-cubic-foot refrigerator. Which woman was known as the Good Queen Bess?"
CONTESTANT: "Bess Truman."

Oh Nurse!

PUBLIC SERVICE ANNOUNCEMENT: "Attention young ladies! Attention young ladies! Your country needs your services. Hospitals throughout the nation are greatly understaffed. Nurses are urgently needed. Volunteer to be one of America's white-clapped ladies of mercy."

Candid Mike

Microphone equipment is becoming smaller and less conspicuous. At a wrestling match, an announcer was busily describing the action in the ring, when he was approached by a wrestling fan.
"It's nice to see we have such a nice crowd here tonight. It's a great turnout; we've got some wonderful matches for you. Now the main event of the evening is gonna be two falls out of three. Chief Bender is going to wrestle with Sando Kovacs—promises to be real exciting. First let's get a word in from our sponsor . . ." (OFF MIKE) "Hey, Mac! Where's the can?"

Lucky Pierre

ANNOUNCER: "It's Music time! Tonight featuring the sounds of Phil Spitoonly . . . Spitalny, and his forty pieces! That is, his all-ghoul orchestra . . . girl orchestra!"

It's What Up Front That Counts

This question was put to the JUVENILE JURY members by moderator Jack Barry: "When you grow up and get married, what would you like your husband or wife to look like?" One five year old said his ideal was Rosemary Clooney, because, he said, "She's got beautiful blue eyes, blonde hair—and a nice body." He added—with gestures—"especially up here . . ."

Cherry Jubilee

KID SHOW: "And for all you kiddies, we are going to dish out cherry ice cream on today's program in celebration of today, February 22nd, George Birthington's Washday!!"

The Cat's Meow

A rock 'n roll disc jockey inadvertently picked up a recording left in his studio by a previous program which featured an hour of concert music. He picked up a recording of a Rachmaninoff concerto and gave it the following introduction. "Now here's a selection that features Rock Maninoff, must be some new cat. Let's give it a listen to."

A New Platform

ANNOUNCER: "This is Station WJSV in Washington, D.C. Pardon me, that's been changed . . . this is Station WTOP in Washington. Stay tuned for PAPLES PLEATFORM which follows over WPOT. That is, PEOPLE'S PLEATFORM."

Stone Face

"Stay stoned for the Rolling Stones . . . next on the 'Ed Sullivan Show'!"

That's My Pop

Qiuz Program: A young lady contestant on NAME THAT TUNE was asked to name a tune which happened to be "Christopher Columbus." The emcee gave her this hint. "If he didn't do what he did, you wouldn't be here today." Her quick answer was—"My father!!"

Practical Joker

Newscaster: "The minister was covered with papers and rubrish, then drenched with kerosene and set afire. The murderer then set the entire house afire . . . More sports after this message from our sponsor."

Quite a Dish

Quiz Program: "Are you ready for your next question? Well, you will be twenty-five dollars richer if you guess the next answer. Remember, if you guess it, our sponsors will send you a twenty-five dollar United States Saving Bond. Now for the question. Russia is famous for its borscht, France is famous for its crepes suzette—now tell me, what famous dish is Hungary noted for?"
Answers "Zsa Zsa Gabor!"

Early Bird

Weather Forecaster: "With the autumn weather now upon us, it seems to be getting early later now!"

Teed Off

"This is Jim Simpson speaking to you from the 18th hole at the National Open. Gardiner Dickenson is getting ready to tee off on this hole, which is 473 years to the green."

Farmer's Daughter

"Final results of the FFA contest are: Apple picking won by Dick Jones. Tractor driving award to Jack Davis. One of our own girls, Miss Betty Smith, was chosen as the best hoer."

The Paws that Refreshes

Poor timing and improper pauses can be the source of many a headache for announcers, as evidenced by the improper change of pace.

". . . And the United Nations will adjourn until next week. And now here's a local news item: A lot of villagers were very startled today when a pack of dogs broke loose from a dog catcher's wagon and raced crazily through the fields of a well known tobacco plantation. . . . Friends, does your cigarette taste different lately?"

What's in a Name?

The microphone is a sensitive instrument and can be dangerous. Listen to this female announcer who forgot the mike was listening.

"And now, audience, here is our special TV Matinee guest that we've all been waiting for—world famous author, lecturer and world traveler, a man about town. Mr. er—er, Mr. . . . Oh! What the hell is his name?"

NBC National Biscuit Company

Bill Garden, Director of Special Events at NBC-TV, recalls an announcer who hurriedly finished a religious program to be in time for a station break. He closed by saying, "Cast thy broad upon the waters." He couldn't finish the quotation in time so he concluded with, "This is the National Breadcasting Company."

Stop-Leak-And Listen

"And that's the weather report from the International Airport here at Anchorage, Alaska. Now I'll take a leak out the window to see if it's freezing outside our studio."

In Front of All These People?

Eddie Peabody, the great banjoist, was introduced thusly:
ANNOUNCER: "Ladies and Gentlemen: Mr. Eddie Playbody will now pee for you."

What's Cookin'?

On a cooking show which originated from a Philadelphia station, a housewife told of a delightful new way "to prepare fricken chicasee."

A Day at the Races

In a broadcast originating from Monmouth Race Track in New Jersey, the announcer was making introductory remarks in preparation for the feature race which was to be run in a few minutes. He was running down the entries when he noticed that the horse which was the favorite, named Harass, was not going to run. He reminded the listener to be sure to scratch Harass!

A Pip

MILTON CROSS: "It's the A&P Program, starring Harry Horlick and his A&G Pippsies."

That's Rich

On "Strike it Rich," popular television program produced by Walt Framer, Warren Hull, Master of Ceremonies, interviewed a five year old child whose father was in the United States Army serving in Korea. She wanted to Strike it Rich for an apartment where she would have her own bedroom; whereupon the surprised Hull asked: "With Daddy away in Korea, isn't the apartment you live in with Mommy big enough?" The child's reply was, "During the week I sleep in the bedroom with Mommy, but on the week-ends, when Uncle Charlie comes, they make me sleep on a cot in the kitchen. Anyway, he's not really my uncle."

Bedtime Story

Performers on all-night telethons get very tired. A perfect example is Morey Amsterdam's appearance on one of these marathons for a worthy cause. Here is what came out, at approximately 3 o'clock in the morning. "Mr. and Mrs. Geilgud of the Bronx sent $2.00. And here's another contribution of $2.00 if you will tell Theresa to go to bed." "All right, Theresa will go to bed for $2.00."

I Wonder What's Become of Sally

"Here's an old favorite—Tenor with organ, *Looking for a Girl Named Sally*."

Scratch Sheet

When Pat Adelman, program director of Station KNOW, Texas, finished preparing the day's schedule, he left it in the control room. Later he made a change—instead of Les Brown's orchestra, he substituted a religious program which was to originate from N. Y. He scratched out Les Brown's and wrote over it, Yom Kippur. When the new announcer came on shift, he picked up the schedule and exhorted his listeners to "Stay tuned for the dance music of Yom Kippur's Orchestra."

Adult Material

EMCEE: "And what do you do for a living, my good lady?"
LADY: "I'm a maid. I do housework, and take care of a large family."
EMCEE: "How large a family?"
LADY: "Well, let's see, there are four boys, three girls, one adult, and one adultress."

Topsy Turvy

On "What's My Line," a program on which occupations are guessed, the contestant was a mattress stuffer. One of the panelists asked this:
"Is your product used by one sex over the other?"

Surprise Party

The following was heard on the "Bride and Groom" radio program.

EMCEE: "And what was the greatest surprise you ever received?"

CONTESTANT: "I got the biggest surprise of my life when my husband came back from the army. I woke up one morning and found him standing by my bed with his discharge in his hands."

Audience roars with laughter.

Quick switch to studio announcer: "There will be a brief pause for organ music."

Tea For Two

"When you're thinking of an all-season thirst quencher, it's a delight—winter or summer—instant White Rose hot or cold Orange Teakoe Pea."

In a Fog

ACTRESS: "The fog was as thick as seepoop."

Small Wonder

"And Dad will love Wonder Bread's delicious flavor too. Remember it's Wonder Bread for the breast in bed."

Parlez-Vous Anglais?

A French Canadian announcer blooped his way through this one.

"This is the Dominion network of the Canadian Broad Corping Castration."

Handy Andy

On *Exploring The Unknown*, a science program, Andre Baruch, reading a commercial for a large corporation called it "the largest producers in the United States of Magnossium, Alleeminum, and Stool."

A Natural

On *Two for the Money*, popular quiz program sponsored by a cigarette company, Herb Shriner, the Indiana Hoosier, asked a contestant, "Are you a natural born citizen of the United States?" "Oh no," the woman replied, "I was born a Caesarean."

A Run for Your Money

"There's excitement in store on our *Million Dollar Movie* tonight with Ann Sheridan—stay tuned as Phillips Milk of Magnesia brings you *Woman on the Run*."

Off Her Crocker

COOKING SHOW: "*Ladies, our baking recipe for today features another delicious Betty Crocker cake mix special . . . and we are sure your entire family will enjoy this Betty Baker crock mix delight.*"

Jack Rabbit

This incident occurred on the *College of Musical Knowledge,* widely-heard musical and audience participation program. The MC was surprised that a lady contestant, young in appearance, had nine children. He asked what her husband did. "Oh! my husband operates an automatic screwing machine!"

Beat the Clock

NARRATOR: ". . . and as his trusty little donkey carried Quixote up the road, he could see the gates of the city ahead. Don Quixote's excitement rose as he contemplated the knightly adventures that awaited him." (*Time running out*) ". . . and there we leave Don Quixote, sitting on his ass, until tomorrow at the same time."

Double Trouble

GANGSTER: "Okay you rat, I've got you covered and now I'm going to drill ya."
(*Complete silence*)
GANGSTER: (*Realizing that the sound effects man has run into trouble*)
"On second thought I'm going to slit your throat."
Two shots—The sound man had located his trouble.

What's Mine Is Mine, What's Yours Is Mine

Senator Austin Warren, in mediating the differences between the Arabs and Israelis at the U.N. came out with this classic. "Now let's all try to settle this problem in a true Christian spirit."

Break the Station

ANNOUNCER: "This is Indiana's first broad-chasing station."

Pocket Pool

A contestant on a quiz program was asked, "What do you find on pool tables that you find in men's trousers?"
The answer should have been pockets.

Foul Play

"Friday is poultry night—remember all ladies present will get a free goose. That is, all ladies will get a goose for free."

He Will Catch the Dickens

"Stay tuned now for a dramatization of Dickens' immortal *Sale of Two Titties*. UH! I mean *Tale of Two Cities*."

Tall Story

QUIZMASTER: "What is the Taj Mahal?"
CONTESTANT: (*After hemming and hawing*) "I'm afraid I don't know."
QUIZMASTER: "I'm awfully sorry, but you should know that the Taj Mahal, located in India, is the greatest erection man has ever had for woman since time immemorial."

Slide, Kelly, Slide

DIZZY DEAN: "The score is tied, and the runners on second and third are taking a lead off their respectable bases. There goes the runner . . . he slud into third base!"

He Blew It

ANNOUNCER: "Yes, there is no doubt that Stephen Foster was one of the greatest, if not the greatest writer of American folk music. His spirituals rank high among the music the world likes best. And now, Stephen Foster's immortal song, 'Old Jack Blow.'"

Strange Interlude

One lesson an announcer learns is to make sure he is off the air before he makes any private comments. But even the greatest sometimes slip. A legend is Uncle Don's remark after he had closed his famous children's program. He thought his mike was cut off the air when he said, "I guess that will hold the little bastards."

12 O'Clock High

Heard on the twelve o'clock news over NBC:
The rumor that President Nixon would veto the bill comes from high White Horse souses.

Just Ducky

COMMENTATOR: "All the world was thrilled with the marriage of the Duck and Doochess of Windsor."

Just Deserts

NEWSCASTER: "Since the G. I. Sergeant James Hermann was refused by the Russians, he has been convicted of desertion, sentenced to three years of hard labor, and been given a desirable discharge."

What's Good for the Goose . . .

"Tune in tomorrow and find out if John will goose Sadie's cook, er I mean, will John cook Sadie's goose?"

Crazy man, Crazy

Let's listen to an introduction of famous news commentator, John Cameron Swayze.
"Stay tuned to John Solomon Cwayze and the news!"

Boomerang

PLAY-BY-PLAY ANNOUNCER: "Here comes the pitch—it's a well-hit ball, going toward straightaway center field . . . going . . . going . . . and it's curving foul!"

Jam Session

While doing research for my television specials, titled "Kermit Schafer's Blunderful World of Bloopers," I came across a Betty Furness Westinghouse refrigerator commercial which occurred on a weekly TV program that I produced on NBC-TV. This was the moment when the refrigerator door got stuck.

When she couldn't get it open on the first two tries, she gritted her teeth and said, "Who's the comedian?" The camera came in close until her face filled the entire screen while she continued the commercial, albeit falteringly. Meantime, the shadows of hands could be seen frantically working on the refrigerator until the camera pulled back showing a doorless, hingeless refrigerator!

Shake Down, I Mean Count Down

NEWSCASTER: "The area around Cape Canaveral has certainly grown in leaps and bounds, largely due to the influx of Army racketeers and their families."

Rumble Seat

Various station cut-ins play havoc with programs heavily laden with commercials, as per this example. "Our lovely model, Susan Dalrymple, is wearing a lovely two-piece ensemble. . . . (STATION CUT-IN) . . . with a rear engine in the back!"

Sam, You Made the Pants Too Long

COMMERCIAL: "Ladies, you will enjoy Sam's department store shopping, which features clothing for the entire family. Our special this week is men's trousers . . . so for the biggest thing in men's trousers . . . come in and see Sam!"

Outstanding Performer

Jimmy Dean, emceeing the TONIGHT SHOW, introduced luscious Abbe Lane thusly: "Abbe Lane is a very beautiful girl with two great things going for her!"

Good Sport

LOCAL NEWS: "That does it for our check on new mothers at Centre County Hospital today. Join us again Monday when we will again present the Sport Report! . . . er . . . Stork Report."

At a Loss for the Right Words

COMMERCIAL: "So remember folks, we have all the latest models in hard tops and convertibles at prices you can't afford to miss. Yes folks, at Courtesy Motors your loss is our gain."

Don't Miss It!

STATION BREAK: "Be sure not to miss THE COMING OF CHRIST, Wednesday, 8:30 P.M., 7:30 Central Time."

Blankety Blank

DISK JOCKEY: "Our all-request recorded program continues with a request from Elmer Peters, who phoned in to please play for my wife who just had a baby at St. Luke's Hospital. . . . 'I DIDN'T KNOW THE GUN WAS LOADED'!!"

I Hear You Calling Massa

MUSICIAN: "For my next selection, I would like to play a medley of Old Stephen Foster favorites; among them will be 'Jeannie with the Light Brown Hair,' 'My Old Kentucky Home,' and 'My Ass Is In The Cold, Cold Ground.' "

Do Not Play with Matches

On a TV Science program, a professor of Physics was experimenting with a gas. At the conclusion of his program, he came up with this classic. "I see our time is running out, and to be on the safe side and before I do anything else, I'll have to ask you to bear with me for a moment while I get rid of my gas!"

Cheese and Crackers!

COMMERCIAL: "Men, when you take your favorite girl out for dinner, atmosphere means an awful lot. You will find the best German food and the best sauerbraten at Joe's Rat Celler . . . er . . . Rathskeller."

Pots and Pans

ANNOUNCER: "We will now hear chamber music from the Potts ensemble!"

Judy, Judy, Judy

DISK JOCKEY: "And now here's an ever-popular favorite, July Garland singing, 'Ding, Ding, Ding Went the Trollop.'"

I Wish I Were Single Again

LOCAL NEWS: "Mr. Baker, who applied for the job, seemed to be very well qualified. He is obviously a man of sound judgment and intelligence. Mr. Baker is not married."

State of the Union

NEWSCASTER: "Judge Walter Thompson warned the manufacturers that the courts had already handed down the decision, and he would look with disfavor upon anyone who tampered with his union suit."

I Ain't Got No Body

SPORTSCASTER: "DiMaggio is back, back, back to the wall, his head hits it, it drops to the ground, he picks it up and throws it to third."

Charge!!!
COMMERCIAL: "Come in at the sign of the clock, where it only takes six months to open a three-minute charge account!"

All Balled Up
DISC JOCKEY: "And that was 'South Town' sung by the Blue Bellies . . . I mean, the Blue Balls . . . the Blue Belles!!"

One-Way Passage
Let's listen to this proud professor of music telling the radio audience about one of his pupils, on a program that originated from a well-known college of music.

"Our next number is Tchaikovsky's violin concerto, featuring our own violin virtuoso, Sol Tannenbaum. You will notice that Mr. Tannenbaum plays passages of ease with the greatest of difficulty."

Figures Do Not Lie
NEWSCASTER: "Our annual report of the committee reveals that health conditions aren't all they should be. The city's beaches have an appalling amount of litter, and a check at the municipal swimming pools reveals some startling figures!"

Stoned
LOCAL NEWS: "And from Mrs. Peyton, President of the Garden Study Club, comes word of a meeting next Friday, There will be a lecture by Eleanor Dayton. The topic of her lecture will be 'My Potted Friends!' "

Little Caesar

On the Texaco Star Theatre, one of the principal actors played a prominent part in the dramatization of Julius Caesar. He had a very important line whereby he was to introduce Bruce Cabot, who was the star of the Shakespearean play. Here is how the introduction came off. "Hail the conquering hero, great leader of armies, renowned figure in history, Sid Caesar!"

Dangerous Curves

SAFETY PROGRAM: "What would you say is the most dangerous room in the house? You would think either the bathroom or the kitchen. Well, here's a surprise. According to a recent study, one fourth of all accidents take place in the bedroom!"

Whoopee!

FASHION COMMENTATOR: "And now for the latest from the fashion world. It is good news for men. Women are not going to wear their dresses any longer . . . this year."

Don't Forget the Sandwiches

SPORTSCASTER: "The broad jump was won by Harry Crawford of Rice University. Pole vault was won by Dick Staley of S.M.U.; the relay race was won by Texas Christian University. And now the event you've all been waiting for, the thousand-mile dash!"

Peek-a-Boo Boo

DISC JOCKEY: "I think the temperature is dropping. While this record is playing I'll go take a leak at the thermometer."

109

Killjoy

COMMERCIAL: "At Gimbels for today only, we are featuring a special on fun-resistant panties . . . I do not mean fun-resistant . . . I mean run-resistant!"

Enjoy, Enjoy

"Good afternoon, this is Hilda Heller, your Garden Club Chairwoman, bringing you another program in our series of useful tips. Today's demonstration will be on 'Hot Beds and Cold Frames,' which I hope you all will enjoy."

Really Convenient

"You will find many attractive features at a Holiday Inn in your area. Holiday Inns are equipped to perform many functions, so when you are thinking of having your next affair, remember a Holiday Inn motel!"

Stop the Music

DISC JOCKEY: "We will continue with our program of uninterrupted music after this message from our sponsor."

Some Choke

PUBLIC SERVICE ANNOUNCEMENT: "So be sure and visit our mobile unit where you can get emphysema free for the asking."

Sleepy Time Gal

Heard on "Secret Storm": "I stayed awake last night dreaming about you."

Some Kind of a Nut

COMMERCIAL: "At Wortman's Furniture store, their interior decorator will give you ideas for your home in every type of wood. Come in today and see their showroom and be their guest in their *walled nut room!*"

111

Honest Abe

COMMERCIAL: "So ladies . : . be sure not to miss our Washington's Birthday special sale on Monday, Lincoln's birthday."

You Can't Tell the Players Without A Score Card

Viewers were watching the exciting Western film titled *Broken Arrows,* which was being presented on "Monday Night at the Movies." A typical scene was being shown where the good guys were huddled around a burning covered wagon shooting frantically at the encircling Apaches, who were getting knocked off with great precision. At this point, superimposed over the action, the following latest football score was shown: "Cowboys 36——Indians 6."

Crop That Out

Heard on station KGO, San Francisco: "And it has been announced that the presidential party will be served the choicest of this year's Lamb *Crap.*"

Jim Dandy

NEWSCASTER: "James Hoffa was scheduled to address prisoners of his Teamsters Union . . . *pensioners!*"

Can the Announcer

"This portion of 'Petticoat Junction' is brought to you by the American Home Company, makers of fine products for your can . . . I mean American *Can* Company . . . makers of fine products for your *home!*"

An American In Paris

"Stay tuned to NBC for developments as the American delegation seeks a peace . . . . spelled p-e-a-c-e . . . . in Paris."

113

Vive la France

On Red Benson's TV Show, NAME THAT TUNE, two contestants, a beautiful French girl and a sailor, were trying for the prize. The orchestra played "The Anniversary Waltz." The beauty said, " 'Oh, How Ve Danced on Ze Nite Ve Vere Ved.' " "No," replied Red, "that's a line from it." Then turning to the sailor he said, "If you were married to this beautiful girl tonight, what would you be singing a year from now?" The sailor replied: " 'Rock-a-bye-Baby!' "

To Err Is Human

EMCEE: "I don't understand . . . a moment ago, you said you had two children . . . now, young lady, you tell me you are not married?"
YOUNG LADY: "Can't a girl make a mistake once in a while?"

Hell to the Chief

HARRY VON ZELL: "Ladies and Gentlemen, the President of the United States, Hoobert Heever."

This concludes . . . this conclees . . . that is all!!!